Setting up a successful jewellery business

Setting up a successful jewellery business

Second Edition

Angie Boothroyd ma(rca)

Clinton Macomb
Public Library

Bloomsbury Academic
An imprint of Bloomsbury Publishing Plc

BLOOMSBURY
LONDON · OXFORD · NEW YORK · NEW DELHI · SYDNEY

Bloomsbury Academic

An imprint of Bloomsbury Publishing Plc

50 Bedford Square	1385 Broadway
London	New York
WC1B 3DP	NY 10018
UK	USA

www.bloomsbury.com

BLOOMSBURY and the Diana logo are trademarks of Bloomsbury Publishing Plc

First edition published in 2011
This edition published in 2017

British Library Cataloguing-in-Publication Data
A catalogue record for this book is available from the British Library.

ISBN:	PB:	978-1-4742-4196-0
	ePDF:	978-1-4742-4197-7
	ePub:	978-1-4742-4198-4

Library of Congress Cataloging-in-Publication Data
A catalogue record for this book is available from the Library of Congress.

Cover design: Sutchinda Thompson

Typeset by Fakenham Prepress Solutions, Fakenham, Norfolk NR21 8NN

Printed and bound in India

To find out more about our authors and books visit www.bloomsbury.com. Here you will find extracts, author interviews, details of forthcoming events and the option to sign up for our newsletters.

Contents

Acknowledgements

Many thanks to everyone who helped make the first and second editions of this book happen: Davida Forbes, Ariadne Goodwin, Molly Beck and Clara Herberg at Bloomsbury, and Susan James at A&C Black (who talked me into the idea in the first place). Thanks to Ellen O'Hara and Janice Hosegood at Cockpit Arts, and to Nigel Jackson who generously provided his wisdom in the area of intellectual property law. Finally, a big thank you to all the jewellers and craftspeople who provided their input and expertise including Alison Flanders, Nicola Monaghan, Selina Stiles, Andrea Kourris, Liz Willis, Sonia Cheadle, Amanda Doughty and Zack Wetherby, and everyone who provided feedback on the first edition in order to make the second edition even better. I sincerely hope that all who read this book benefit from the combined expertise of these and other people who have directly or indirectly contributed.

Introduction

Who is this book for?

This book is for anyone who designs and makes jewellery and wants to earn money doing it. If you are just setting up your business and don't know where to start when it comes to pricing, selling or promoting your work, then this is an ideal place to learn. Or maybe you're already an established designer/maker, but aren't entirely confident of your business skills? Perhaps you juggle a jewellery business alongside another job or career? If so, this book is also perfectly suited to your needs.

Whether you want to sell directly to the public, or through shops and galleries, this book will give you the tools you need to help you price, promote and sell your work.

It will also be helpful if you are considering opening a retail premises. However, it does not cover the complicated business of opening a shop; for that, you will also need a book specifically aimed at shopkeepers, of which there are many on the market.

If you are a jewellery designer but not a maker, and plan on outsourcing the manufacture of your products, you will also find this book useful, although some chapters will not apply directly to you. A look at the chapter headings will show you how you will benefit.

What to expect

This book is not about making jewellery. It's about turning your jewellery into a successful business. It is largely based on my personal experience, and therefore addresses many unwritten rules and industry-specific guidelines that you won't find in more general business books. All the fundamental skills required to run a small jewellery business are included here, along with worksheets so you can put what you've learned into practice.

About the author

My first career was in graphic design. After three years working for a design studio I knew I had the confidence, and the design skills, to strike out on my own. Sadly, I knew nothing about business. I ended up working harder than ever before, for less money, and on increasingly mundane projects. The business was ultimately a failure.

I retrained as a jeweller, first doing a technical course and then completing a Master of Arts at the Royal College of Art. Having decided to become self-employed yet again, I set up my workshop immediately after graduating, and it was a success. Why? This time, I knew a bit about business. Only a little, but it went a long way.

Towards the end of the MA programme we spent a few days discussing professional practice – in other words, business. I can clearly recall the day that a guest speaker came in to explain how to create a cash flow forecast; it was a revelation. I couldn't believe I'd attempted to run a business for years without ever using this powerful, yet basic, business tool. No wonder I'd failed!

After graduating, I carried on educating myself at every opportunity. When I first set up my workshop there were many seminars in London, aimed at helping new craft businesses to get started. I made a habit of attending these, and did so until I felt I had collected the essential business knowledge I needed to survive. Of course, I was simultaneously learning on the job. And because I'd made friends with lots of other jewellers, both at college and in neighbouring studios, I learned a lot from them as well.

And so, with this book, I have attempted to distil all of my education, whether from formal seminars, personal experience or chance conversations, into a concise and easy-to-use volume.

How to use this book

If you are starting a business from scratch, then please read through the entire book before you do anything else. Chapters inevitably cross-reference each other, and everything will make much more sense once you have digested it as a whole.

If you are already in business you may wish to jump into the chapters that are of particular relevance to you, but – of course – I would advise you to read the entire book at some point, as you may just stumble on some hidden gems you didn't know you were looking for.

At the back of the book, you'll also find an appendix of companies, people, associations and exhibitions which I hope will serve as a useful reference tool for years to come.

1 Getting started

So, you've decided to start a jewellery business. Whether it's going to be full-time or part-time, whether operating from a fully-fitted workshop or your garage or kitchen table, there are certain basics you need to take care of at the outset.

First steps

Decide on a legal structure

In legal terms, there are several types of business. Most designer/makers set up as sole traders; in other words, they are self-employed. If you are setting up a business with somebody else, you will need to form a partnership, or you may choose to trade as a limited company. It is always best to seek the advice of an accountant on this subject, as they can advise on the most suitable and tax-efficient structure for you; if you are considering anything other than a simple sole proprietorship, you will certainly need an accountant's advice. Also refer to the small business advice section of your government's website for further information.

FIND THE LATEST INFORMATION ON YOUR GOVERNMENT WEBSITE:

UK: www.gov.uk

USA: www.irs.gov/businesses/small

EUROPE: ec.europa.eu/internal_market/eu-go/index_en.htm

AUSTRALIA: www.business.gov.au

The options for the legal structure of your business will vary slightly, depending on your country of residence, but they are likely to include:

SOLE TRADER

Most makers choose this option as it is the most straightforward. All you need to do is to inform the government of your sole-trader status, and start trading. In the US (where it is also called sole proprietorship), most states will ask you to file a 'fictitious name certificate' if the name of your business is something other than your own name. Probably the biggest drawback to being a sole trader is the fact that your business and personal assets are considered as one in the eyes of the law. In other words, if your business were to go bust, you would be personally liable, and therefore your personal assets could be at risk.

PARTNERSHIP

A partnership is still relatively straightforward in that it consists of two or more self-employed people running a business together. Again, personal and business assets are not legally separate, so there is a risk to your personal possessions if the business fails.

LIMITED LIABILITY PARTNERSHIP

This is similar to a partnership but with added legal protection in terms of how much finance each partner has contributed to the business.

LIMITED LIABILITY COMPANY

If you set up a company, you are not self-employed, but an employee of your company. The main reason people choose this option is that it separates their personal finances from those of their business, so their personal assets enjoy a level of protection which would not be possible if they were self-employed. Running a company does carry extra costs; aside from the cost of registering the company, you will also incur extra fees with your accountant on an ongoing basis. Once you reach a certain level of income, however, these fees are more than offset by tax savings.

Choose a trading name

If you are a sole trader, your trading name will normally just be your name: 'Mary Smith' or 'Joe Bloggs'. Don't worry if your name is not particularly memorable or glamorous; it will become so by association with your jewellery. If you have a reason to call your business something other than your own name then, by all means, go ahead. But don't complicate matters for the sake of it.

If you are going into partnership with somebody, then you will need to devise a trading name. Don't be afraid to simply put your surnames together in the time-honoured 'Smith and Bloggs' format.

Inform the government

You need to inform the government that you're starting a business. This applies even if you are continuing with full-time work and starting your business in your spare time. Your government website should provide information about how to register as self-employed. For other legal structures, your accountant will probably need to take care of the paperwork for you.

Be prepared to invest in your business

In order to make money, it is inevitable that you will need to spend money. You will need not only your tools and your materials but you will soon find the everyday expenses piling up too – stationery supplies, software, postage and the like. In order to estimate how much cash you'll need to get started you would be wise to produce a cash flow forecast. (See pages 115–20 for details of how to do this.) If you haven't got the cash to finance the business yourself, you may be able to find funding. A good place to start is by contacting your local professional association (see pages 141–2) who may be able to advise you on funding specifically for jewellery designers or craftspeople in general. Failing that, you can always finance your business with a bank loan. Ask your accountant for advice; they may be able to point you in the right direction while also advising you on the most tax-efficient form of borrowing for you.

Open a business bank account

No matter what the legal structure of your business, it needs a dedicated bank account. This doesn't technically have to be a business bank account if you are trading under your own name; it could be just a second personal account. (Business accounts often come with hefty fees, for a service no different to that offered to personal customers.) Most jewellers do, however, run a proper business bank account. Do your research, as fees vary widely. If you're lucky, you'll find one that's free – or almost free.

Find out about tax

INCOME TAX

You must pay income tax. When you inform the government of your business intentions, make sure you find out what your tax obligations are. If it's too complicated for you to cope with, get an accountant. They will usually save you more money than they cost, and the peace of mind is priceless.

SALES TAX

Your government website should also be able to tell you whether you are obliged to charge sales tax. This will vary from country to country. At the time of writing, if you are based in the UK and your turnover is above £83,000, you must become VAT-registered and therefore charge 20 per cent Value Added Tax on all your sales of jewellery within the UK. (The rules for selling outside the UK are a bit more complicated.) In the US, tax laws vary from state to state. Go online and familiarize yourself with your local tax laws before you start trading.

Get a hallmark

In the UK, and in most of Europe, it is illegal to describe a piece of jewellery for sale as being made of silver, gold or any other precious metal, unless it carries an official hallmark. (Exemption applies to items below a certain weight.) So, if you use precious metals in your work, you must have it hallmarked. This means submitting it to an assay office where it will be tested and stamped.

In the US, your work does not legally require a hallmark. However, consumers will often look for a fineness stamp (e.g. 14

Carat or karat?

There are two different concepts covered by these words. One refers to the purity of gold; the other is a unit of measure used to weigh gemstones.

The purity of gold is expressed in parts out of 24. Pure gold is referred to as being 24 karat (in the US) or carat (in the UK). 18 carat gold is 18/24ths gold – in other words, 75 per cent.

The weight of gemstones is measured in carats, but this kind of carat (always spelled with a 'c') is a fixed unit of weight, and is equal to 200 milligrams.

karat, 18 karat) on your jewellery. You can buy these stamps from your tool dealer.

If you are based in the UK, refer to page 147 for a list of assay offices. Register with the one nearest to you.

What you absolutely need

Somewhere to work

Finding a suitable workshop can be tricky. You need not only a bench space, but somewhere you feel comfortable designing, experimenting and taking care of paperwork. You are likely to spend at least half your time on administrative tasks, so, no matter how small your business, you will probably want a dedicated space for this.

WORKING FROM HOME

If you are on a tight budget and are fortunate enough to have the space, working from home can be a sensible option. Apart from the cost savings, you'll also benefit from the lack of a commute. It's also a popular choice for people who need to balance their designing and making with other commitments such as childcare or other work.

On the downside, you may come to regret the lack of separation between work and home life. It can be very difficult to relax at home when the workshop beckons, only a few feet away. There is also the noise to consider: if you do a lot of hammering, for example, will the neighbours be affected? There may also be health and safety regulations to consider, such as restrictions on the use of hazardous chemicals or compressed gases in the home. Consider your clients too. Do you want to welcome them into your home, or would you prefer to keep your private life private?

Planning regulations and covenants on some properties may also prohibit you from running a business from home or restrict what you can do.

RENTING A WORKSHOP

Renting a workshop creates a clear delineation between work and home life, as well as giving a more professional appearance to the business. Noise and chemicals are not normally a cause for concern in an industrial environment, and you may also find you work more productively without the distractions of home. All this comes at a price, of course, and this will vary widely depending on the location and type of workshop that you choose.

SHARED WORKSHOPS

You may be able to find workshops which have been set up specially for jewellers, or for craftspeople in general. In such spaces, it is common for several businesses to share one workshop. Depending on how the studios are run, sharing may be something organized by the craftspeople themselves, or perhaps administered by a studio manager (who may be based in a central office). You may find yourself sharing space with other jewellers, in which case you may be able to reach an agreement on the communal use of tools and machinery. Or you might end up sharing with makers from other disciplines, which can be useful in other ways. Whatever your situation, you want to be sure that you are compatible with your fellow craftspeople not only personally but also in terms of your work practices. Do you all have similar tolerance levels for noise, dust and smelly chemicals?

Many shared spaces come with additional benefits, such as 'open studio' events, whereby the whole building is open to the public for a weekend. This can be a great way of building your client base and making sales, all without the hassle of carting your showcases off to an exhibition. Some workshops are run as charities and as such also provide a range of business support for makers, such as seminars and one-to-one business advice.

The benefits of sharing are not just limited to practical concerns. In an open workshop environment there is generally a culture of mutual support and encouragement, which you may miss if you decide to work in isolation in your own space. If you are a sociable creature and enjoy the banter of a busy workplace, then you would be well advised to seek out a space that is shared with other jewellers, craftspeople or in fact any other discipline that is compatible in practical terms. You may also find that unexpected opportunities arise just by being in contact with other people on a daily basis; you never know where your next client or contact might come from.

There is a list of workspace providers on page 147 to help get you started. You may also want to contact your local jewellery or craft associations for advice; you can find these on pages 141–2.

Computer

It hardly needs saying that you will need a computer and internet connection if you are to keep pace with your competitors. Ideally, you'll want a lightweight, portable device so that you can take care of business while on the move, or at exhibitions.

Digital camera / smartphone

Although there will be times when professional photography is called for, you will need a way of documenting your work digitally. You may even be able to get away with taking your own pictures for web and print if you have the time and inclination to get it right.

Business cards

In the jewellery business it is standard for people to have postcards with images of their work, or business cards with full-colour photos on the back. There are several companies who offer inexpensive, small runs of good-quality business cards online, so these don't need to break the bank.

Finding your niche

As a jewellery designer you should make it your business to cultivate a knowledge of current trends and movements within the industry – in other words, to carry out market research. The term might sound dry and analytical, but market research can be anything but that. Going to see jewellery at exhibitions, galleries and shops is crucial to maintaining an awareness of the field, and should become an ongoing part of your work. After all, to contribute usefully to any subject, you should have a current knowledge of it.

But first, you should try to have a sense of where your jewellery sits in the grand scheme of things. The jewellery world is vast and diverse, and knowing where you fit in will help guide your business decisions along the way.

Different types of jewellery

If you are new to jewellery, this is a good time to think about how your work might be described in terms of genre. There are dozens, if not hundreds, of niches within niches. I've done my best to define the main areas here, but I do not wish to create delineations. These are all flexible definitions with a lot of overlap between them. They are meant only as a rough guide to help broaden your awareness of jewellery in its wider context, so that you can better understand where your work fits in.

Studio jewellery

There are at least half a dozen terms for this, and I had a hard time deciding which one would get headline status here, but 'studio jewellery' seems to roll off the tongue most easily. It refers to jewellery created by individuals who have developed their own unique working methods and/or artistic styles. It encompasses both business-focused designers making multiple pieces in traditional metals such as silver and gold, and conceptual artists making jewellery art pieces in unconventional and unexpected materials. The handmade nature of studio jewellery has traditionally been a key factor, but many artists now make use of digital technology in their work. Other tags used are 'fine art jewellery', 'art jewellery', 'wearable art', 'contemporary jewellery', 'craft jewellery' and 'artisan jewellery'. (And remember that in the US, it's always spelled 'jewelry'.) In the UK, artists working in this way are on the whole referred to as 'designer/makers'.

Designer jewellery

The meaning of this term seems to have shifted in recent years, with the explosion of new jewellery galleries and shops. It used to be similar to studio jewellery, but now seems to have taken on a more commercial meaning. Even global jewellery manufacturers now refer to their jewellery as 'designer'.

Fashion jewellery

Fashion jewellery changes with the fashion seasons, so if you work in this arena you will typically be coming out with a new collection every six months. The disposable nature of fashion jewellery means it is made from non-precious materials, but it can include silver, which is still relatively inexpensive compared with gold or platinum. Fashion jewellery is also sometimes referred to as 'costume jewellery'.

Precious jewellery

This is a term applied to any jewellery made from precious metals or stones. It may be traditional or contemporary in design. Typical materials are gold, platinum, diamonds and other precious and semi-precious stones. Another term for this is 'fine jewellery', although this tends to refer to more traditional designs, especially using precious stones, which is called 'fine gem-set jewellery'.

NON-PRECIOUS JEWELLERY

Predictably, this is jewellery made from non-precious materials. These could be base metals, plastics, aluminium, in fact anything other than precious metals and stones. Non-precious does not mean cheap, however; although art jewellery is often made from non-precious materials, its value resides in its artistic merit rather than intrinsic material worth. Fashion jewellery is a type of non-precious jewellery.

Conducting market research

Being aware of the general state of the jewellery industry is a good starting point, but there will be times when you need to conduct more analytical research to answer specific questions.

IDENTIFY YOUR QUESTIONS

Your research will be much more constructive if you set out to answer specific questions, such as:

- Who is your competition?
- Are there products out there that are similar to yours, in terms of appearance, use of materials, design or price point?
- Why would somebody choose your jewellery over that of your competitors, or vice versa?
- Is there a gap in the market that you could fill?
- In which shops can you envisage your work?

FIND THE ANSWERS

With your questions firmly in your hand, the next step is to venture out to find the answers to them. Don't succumb to doing all your research online – there's no substitute for real life.

TRADE FAIRS

These are a great way to get a snapshot of the entire industry at any given time. Not only will you see everyone's latest collections and, if you're lucky, their prices, but you will also get a feel for the general vibe of the industry. Consult pages 142–3 for a list of fairs to visit.

RETAIL FAIRS

Here you can often meet designer/makers who sell their work directly to the public. Be respectful of the privacy of any designers you speak to. They pay a lot of money to be at these fairs and will not be keen to share their trade secrets with a stranger, nor will they appreciate you taking up their time while a queue of genuine customers forms behind you. Retail prices are often displayed at such events, so you can learn a lot from just looking.

MAGAZINES

Consumer glossies such as *Vogue* and *Tatler* give increasing space to jewellery these days, so it is worth buying a few of these monthly. Cut out any jewellery images that have either a) a similar look and feel to yours, b) use similar materials to yours, or c) have a similar design ethos. Then, every few months or so, compile them into groups. Wherever possible, include prices. Make them into a collage to form a snapshot of what is currently on the market. How do your prices compare? Where are these pieces selling? Could you approach the buyers from these shops?

ONLINE

This may be the lazy person's approach to market research, but it works. Use the internet, but don't let it become a substitute for experiencing the world first hand.

THE MYSTERY SHOP

This is my favourite method of market research. It's direct, straight to the point, and fun (provided you are comfortable with it). Say, for example, you have designed a gold necklace, and you want to see what similar necklaces are already on the market, to get an idea of where your piece compares in terms of design and price. Go into a shop where you imagine this could be sold. Be anonymous, obviously – this is a mystery shop, after all.

Pretend that you are buying a gold necklace for your mother's 60th birthday, or that you and some friends from work are chipping in to buy a leaving present for your boss, or that you're buying a treat for yourself. If a sales assistant offers to help, explain the occasion and what you're looking for. Really put yourself in the position of the customer. Convince yourself that you really are buying this gold necklace.

Take notes, just as you would if you really were researching for an important present. How do the different designs compare in terms of design and price? Which piece is your favourite? Apart from the design, are you happy with the length, the clasp mechanism, the weight? Do any unexpected concerns arise?

Politely thank the assistant for their help, and go home and think about what you've just seen. If your necklace had been in the shop, would you, the customer, have been tempted to buy it? If not, why not? What impact might your findings have on your work?

2 Pricing your jewellery

There is probably no greater source of anxiety for the jewellery designer than putting a price on a piece. Too high and it will never sell, while underpricing could mean losing potential profit, or even making a loss. Your livelihood, your reputation and your sanity all depend on getting this number right.

Pricing a piece: The method

If done correctly, pricing is easy. The reason it is problematic for most jewellers is that they don't know where to start, so just end up pulling numbers out of thin air. The ensuing anxiety is understandable.

To know what to charge for a piece, you must first answer some questions about your business. Only then can you effectively price your work in a way that you know will be profitable. This may not make a lot of sense right now, but all will soon be clear.

Commission-only jewellers:

If you plan to work solely on a commission basis for private clients, the rules for pricing are a bit different. Notes for you are included throughout this chapter; also refer to the section 'Commission-only jewellers' on pages 43–4.

Calculate your hourly rate: The magic formula

To price your work, you first need to know what your hourly rate is. It is tempting to just ask around and see what everyone else is charging, and then follow suit. This is fine as a form of research, but as a method for setting your own hourly rate it could be catastrophic.

DETERMINE YOUR ANNUAL OVERHEADS

You first need to undertake what may seem a rather daunting task, and that is estimating your annual overheads. I will do everything I can to guide you through the process with minimal discomfort, but you may have to face a few hard facts about the costs of running a business.

Your overheads are the costs that your business will incur whether you make a single piece of jewellery or not – in other words, expenses that are required just to keep your business running. The rent, for example, always has to be paid, regardless of whether or not you use your workshop. Your general stationery expenses will remain fairly constant too, as will your insurance bills, web-hosting fees and so on.

Elements of the business which are definitely not overheads would be the cost of materials, and production services such as polishing and stone-setting. These costs vary directly in line with how much jewellery you produce and do not feature in this exercise. Ignore them for the time being. Such expenses are referred to as 'Cost of Sales' or 'Cost of Goods Sold'.

WORKSHEET: YOUR ANNUAL OVERHEADS

There is a worksheet on page 29 for you to fill in with your own estimated overheads. I've listed several categories of costs you are likely to incur, and you should ignore any that don't apply to you. Don't get too hung up on the categories themselves; they are provided as a guide. What's important is the sum total of all these expenses. Remember, these are your annual overheads, for an entire year. It doesn't matter if jewellery is your full-time occupation or if you are running it part-time alongside another job, just include all the expenses related to your jewellery business for the period of one year.

Notes are included below to help you work your way through the list. If you feel completely at sea, rest assured that everyone who's ever started a business probably felt the same way. By undertaking this exercise you'll be better prepared than most, even if it's not 100 per cent accurate. Just make the best guesses that you can, and err on the side of caution by overestimating your expenses if you're unsure.

RENT; HEAT AND POWER; TELEPHONE AND INTERNET: These only apply if you are planning on renting a workshop space. If you're using a room in your house or setting aside a space in the garage, no additional expense will be incurred. (Your home telephone bill might be affected, though, so enter any additional telephone expense here.)

INSURANCE: If anyone other than you is going to set foot inside your premises, or if you plan to exhibit at jewellery fairs, you will probably need public liability insurance. You should also insure your stock (your jewellery) and your tools and equipment, just as you would your personal belongings. There are specialist insurers for the jewellery industry but their policies are often more than are required for a start-up business. Look online for insurers offering smaller policies for craftspeople as these might be more appropriate.

MOTOR EXPENSES: Include any motor-related expenses here that will result from the business, including petrol for any long-distance travel.

PRINTED STATIONERY, BROCHURES: This includes business cards, postcards, letterheads and any promotional literature you might need. If you need the design work done for you, include that cost here too.

GENERAL OFFICE SUPPLIES: This is a cost that is higher in the first few years of business as you slowly build your office essentials; you will probably find yourself ordering stationery supplies on a monthly basis, so be careful not to underestimate this.

PHOTOGRAPHY: You will need a minimum of six professional-quality photographs of your jewellery for fair application forms; you will certainly want to have at least one batch of picture postcards printed using one of these images as well.

MARKETING, ADVERTISING: You may get away without spending much on these areas. Technically, exhibitions come under this category but I've given them their own line as they are such a major expense.

WEBSITE: This can be anything from a single-page, self-build website to a professionally designed and built online shop.

EXHIBITIONS: Fairs are expensive. Remember the quoted stand fee usually does not include electricity, lights or showcases. Also, don't forget the cost of travel and accommodation if the event is not a local one.

PACKAGING: There are dozens of companies specializing in jewellery packaging; be sure to find out what the minimum order quantities are and what the artwork set-up fees are.

POSTAGE, SHIPPING: Include day-to-day postage expenses as well as courier costs.

TRAVEL AND SUBSISTENCE: Journeys to research exhibitions, shops, or to meet prospective customers – any business-related travel expenses, including all those coffees along the way. (If I'm exhibiting at a fair I'll put all my related travel expenses under 'Exhibitions'.)

LOOSE TOOLS: Needle files, saw blades, bottled gas, general workshop consumables.

BANK CHARGES: Charges relating to your business bank account, as well as your merchant account (for taking credit card payments) if you have one.

PROFESSIONAL FEES: With any luck this will just be an annual bill from your accountant.

DRAWINGS: This is what you pay yourself. Get used to the idea that your salary is a business expense like any other. Just as you have to pay the rent every month, you should pay yourself too by setting up a standing order from your business account to your personal account.

DETERMINE YOUR ANNUAL PROFITABLE MAKING HOURS

Time for a change of gear now; for this next section you won't be thinking about money at all. This is all about that other elusive commodity – time.

During your business day you will spend some of your time, but not all of it, making jewellery. By 'making' I mean actual cutting, filing, soldering and so on. These are what I will call your 'making hours'.

You will also spend a lot of time, probably more than you think, taking care of administrative duties: paying bills, buying materials, writing press releases, not to mention the hundreds of other unexpected tasks that will inevitably crop up. These I'll call 'admin hours'. Because this time is not directly linked to specific pieces of jewellery, you will not be directly billing your customers for these hours.

Don't be confused by the term 'admin'. Here, it encompasses more than just paperwork, and can refer to just about anything that falls outside the term 'making'. For example, building a workbench in your new workshop, taking your laptop in for repair, designing

WORKSHEET: YOUR ANNUAL OVERHEADS

☐ ACTUAL
☐ PREDICTED

YEAR [   ]

Rent [   ]

Heat, power [   ]

Telephone and Internet [   ]

Insurance [   ]

Motor expenses [   ]

Printed stationery, brochures [   ]

General office supplies [   ]

Photography [   ]

Marketing, advertising [   ]

Website [   ]

Exhibitions [   ]

Packaging [   ]

Postage, shipping [   ]

Travel and subsistence [   ]

Loose tools [   ]

Bank charges [   ]

Professional fees [   ]

Drawings [   ]

Other 1 _____ [   ]

Other 2 _____ [   ]

Other 3 _____ [   ]

Other 4 _____ [   ]

TOTAL ANNUAL OVERHEADS [   ]

NOTES

custom Christmas cards to send to your clients – all of these tasks and many more fall into the admin category. If it's work, but it's not making, then it's admin. Even design time counts as admin for the purpose of this exercise.

Commission-only jewellers: you will probably want to include your design time in your 'making hours' as you will most likely bill your customers directly for this.

WORKSHEET: YOUR ANNUAL PROFITABLE MAKING HOURS

The next step is to determine how many hours a year you will spend on actual making. More specifically, making work that will actually sell. Follow the guidelines below and fill in the worksheet on page 32.

HOURS PER WEEK SPENT ON THE BUSINESS: Will you work a traditional 40-hour week? That would mean 9 a.m. – 6 p.m. if you take an hour for lunch. Is this going to be your full-time occupation or will you be balancing it with other, part-time work? It's completely up to you. Don't feel restricted by convention; if you only have 10 hours a week to commit to your business, that's fine. The important thing is that it's all in the plan. Remember, this figure includes both making and admin hours.

WORKING WEEKS PER YEAR: How many weeks do you plan on working each year? Remember to give yourself at least one holiday. You're the boss, so make it as long or as short as you want, within reason. Also allow for at least a week of sick leave.

WORKING HOURS PER YEAR: Multiply your figures from the top two boxes to arrive at your total working hours per year. For example, if you plan on working 35 hours per week, for 47 weeks of the year, you would calculate 35 x 47, giving you 1,645 total working hours.

PERCENTAGE OF HOURS SPENT MAKING: As a percentage, what proportion of your time do you think you'll spend on making? As a rule, it is safe to say that you will spend more time on admin than you think. If you are unsure, I would suggest that your making hours are likely to fall somewhere between 40 per cent and 60 per cent.

ANNUAL MAKING HOURS: Multiply your figures from boxes C and D. For example, if your total working hours are 1,645 and your making hours are at 60 per cent, that would give you a result of 987. This is an important figure. It is the total number of hours you will spend making jewellery in a year.

PERCENTAGE OF YOUR STOCK THAT WILL BE SOLD DURING THE YEAR: It would be great if every piece of jewellery you made resulted in a sale. This is, however, unlikely, unless you work only to commission. For this reason you need to adjust your annual making hours figure to reflect the number of hours that will actually result in sales during your first year in business. It's not easy, but take a guess. If your jewellery is reasonably well received, this figure could be around 70 per cent. If you work only to commission, then this figure should in theory be 100 per cent.

(Note: In future years this step may not be necessary, as you will have leftover stock from previous years. The old stock that sells will balance out the new stock that doesn't, and you may find that all your making hours are essentially profitable. So, if your business is already established, you can also enter 100 per cent here.)

ANNUAL PROFITABLE MAKING HOURS: Multiply your box E figure by the percentage in box F. The result is the number of hours that you expect to translate directly into sales. As an example, if you are making for 987 hours a year, and 60 per cent of your work is sold, you then have a figure of 592.2 profitable making hours, which you would then round off to a more digestible 592. This is an important figure as it will form the basis of your entire pricing structure.

Maths refresher: Percentages

To calculate a percentage:

To determine, for example, 60 per cent of 987, you can calculate either:

987 x 0.60

or

987 x 60/100

WORKSHEET: YOUR ANNUAL PROFITABLE MAKING HOURS

	A [ ]	Hours per week spent on the business
x	B [ ]	Working weeks per year
=	C [ ]	Working hours per year
x	D [%]	Percentage of hours spent making
=	E [ ]	Annual making hours
x	F [%]	Percentage of your stock that will be sold during the year
=	G [ ]	Annual profitable making hours

DETERMINE YOUR HOURLY RATE

This is where all the numbers come together.

You now know what your annual overheads are (or you've at least made your best guess), so you know how much money you need to bring into the business each year to keep it running.

You also know (roughly) how many hours you will spend each year making jewellery that will sell.

Those profitable making hours need to bring in enough money to cover your overheads. The following simple formula will ensure this.

WORKSHEET: YOUR HOURLY RATE

ANNUAL OVERHEADS: Take your total annual overheads figure from the worksheet on page 29 and enter it in box A on the following page.

ANNUAL PROFITABLE MAKING HOURS: Enter your box G figure from the worksheet above.

HOURLY RATE: Take box A and divide by box B. For example, if your annual overheads are £30,000 and your annual profitable making hours come to 800, then your hourly rate would be £37.50. This figure represents the absolute minimum that you can charge per hour that you work.

WORKSHEET: YOUR HOURLY RATE

[A]	Annual overheads
÷ [B]	Annual profitable making hours
= [C]	HOURLY RATE

Pricing a piece of jewellery

This is where all your carefully crafted numbers are finally put to good use. The worksheet on page 36 will help you to determine your price for any piece of work. Feel free to photocopy it as many times as you like for your own use.

Go through this worksheet using a piece you have previously made as an example. If it's something you've already sold, great. It will be interesting to compare the selling price with the figure you arrive at here. If you haven't yet sold the piece, that's even better. Think about what you would expect it to sell for in a shop or online, or to a private client you may know. Then see how your proposed price measures up against the cold, hard facts. Write in pencil as you'll want to try out a few variations, especially when it comes to mark-ups.

WORKSHEET: PRICING A PIECE OF JEWELLERY

Put simply, pricing is just a matter of this simple idea: Cost + Profit = Price. The worksheet (page 36) is therefore divided into these three sections.

COSTS

The first aspect of costs to consider is your labour. Carefully add up the hours spent making the piece and make notes in the box provided. Remember, 'making' refers to the physical making of jewellery. Unless you work solely to commission, do not include time spent on design, as this is accounted for in your 'admin hours'. Likewise, do not include other tasks such as delivering work to your setter or polisher, or hours spent queuing up to buy materials.

It is a good idea to note down as much detail as possible here, as you may want to refer to these notes in future should you find yourself needing to provide a quote on a similar piece.

Underneath the box, fill in the blanks with your total hours and your hourly rate (from box C on the previous page). Multiply these to arrive at your labour costs and write this amount in box A.

The next box is where you list your costs for materials and services. Note these down individually. Do not add any mark-up just yet. Materials might include gold, silver and gemstones; services would typically be things such as setting, polishing and hallmarking. Do not include indirect costs such as the amount of propane you think might have been used in soldering; indirect costs such as this are accounted for in your overheads so can safely be ignored here. Add up your materials and services costs and enter them in box B.

A note about tax: (Tax laws vary widely from country to country so I will only provide a general explanation here.) If you are tax registered, then exclude any taxes from your material costs here. The tax you charge to your customers will be added later.

Add your box A and B figures to arrive at your total costs, which go in box C.

PROFIT

Profit is the amount added to your costs so that your business makes money – in other words, more money than just the bare minimum required to keep it running. How much profit you decide on may require a bit of trial and error. In box D, enter a percentage at which to mark up your costs. The size of your mark-up will depend largely on your particular type of jewellery and the market in your country. For example, while it is common for makers to double the cost of their gold and silver, the market would not withstand such a high profit on a large diamond. (This is the result of the internet; the public now has access to websites that sell diamonds to the public at near-wholesale prices. The public do not, however, have easy access to gold sheet and wire prices, so have nothing to compare your prices to, except other jewellery, which is not a straightforward like-for-like comparison.)

I would suggest entering a profit of around 40 per cent in box D, just as a starting point. You can always change it later. If this is your first year in business, your profit might have to be lower. This is because those extra overheads associated with starting up a business will make your hourly rate relatively high, and putting a big mark-up on materials might make your work too expensive.

Use this worksheet to experiment. Whatever you do, don't take your profit right down to zero. You need at least 15 per cent for contingency reasons – in other words, to account for mistakes, cost fluctuations and other unexpected charges you may incur.

However, you may want to add up the costs of any large diamonds separately and apply a smaller profit to them, perhaps 10 per cent or so. The choice is ultimately up to you, and will be informed by what the current market will bear.

Take your box D figure and multiply this by your total costs from box C. The resulting profit goes in box E. For example, if your total costs came to £200 and you'd chosen a profit of 40 per cent, your box E figure would be £80.

PRICE

Price is simply a matter of cost plus profit, so the next step is to add your costs from box C and your profit from box E. Enter the result in box F. This is your wholesale price. (Commission-only jewellers, this will be your one and only price, your retail price.)

Now for yet another mark-up. In box G you are going to enter your retail mark-up to arrive at your retail price. I have not included a percentage sign here. This is because retail mark-ups are usually expressed in terms such as '2.5' or '3' rather than in percentages.

Again, this varies not only between countries but from city to city. In London, mark-ups of 3 are commonplace, but in the north of England 2 or 2.5 is more typical. In Tokyo, mark-ups of 4 are not unusual. You will want to add a mark-up that is typical for your area, or for the area where your work will be sold. This will be the retail price that you charge the public when they buy directly from you. It is also the price at which shops will be likely to sell your work when they buy it from you at wholesale and add their mark-up.

Be aware of tax. In the UK, retail prices include sales tax (VAT). In the US, they do not; tax is added at the till. Whether the retail prices you quote to the public are inclusive or exclusive of tax, just make sure they comply with the law and are in line with the norm.

If you don't know what level of mark-up is typical for your area, just enter a figure somewhere between 2 and 3 in box G. Start with 2.5 and see where that gets you.

Now multiply your wholesale price from box F by your retail mark-up in box G. So, if your wholesale price is £280 and your mark-up is 2.3, you would enter £644 in box H. I've called this

WORKSHEET: PRICING A PIECE OF JEWELLERY

TITLE / DESCRIPTION

DATE

COSTS

LABOUR: NOTES AND BREAKDOWN OF MAKING HOURS

_____ HOURS @ _____ / HOUR = LABOUR COST OF

A

MATERIALS AND SERVICES: NOTES AND BREAKDOWN OF COSTS

MATERIALS AND SERVICES COST

B

(BOX A + BOX B)

C

TOTAL COSTS

PROFIT

D
              %

PROFIT

(BOX C x BOX D)

E

PROFIT

PRICE

(BOX C + BOX E)

F

WHOLESALE PRICE

G

RETAIL MARKUP

(BOX F x BOX G)

H

THEORETICAL
RETAIL PRICE

_(TAKE BOX H AND
ROUND OFF)_

J

RETAIL PRICE

NOTES:

your 'theoretical' retail price because it is likely to be an awkward number. (When was the last time you saw a piece of jewellery priced at £644?) Round this number up or down slightly to get a more reasonable figure in box J. If it were me, I'd call it £650.

Troubleshooting pricing

So, you've priced up a piece of jewellery – in theory. How do you feel? Relieved? Shocked? Incredulous?

If you have calculated a retail price which is lower than the one you were expecting, consider yourself lucky; you've got room for manoeuvre. If, on the other hand, you've arrived at a price higher than what you had hoped for, join the club. This is the more usual scenario.

Whether your price seems too low or too high, you will probably want to make some kind of adjustment after completing your pricing worksheet. Even if your calculations deliver a price which seems about right, it is a good idea to consider the factors discussed in this section, as this will help you to understand your pricing in context.

WHAT TO DO IF YOUR PRICES SEEM TOO HIGH

I remember when I was first taught this pricing formula in my very last week on a practical jewellery course. We'd all worked for years honing our skills, many of us hoping to start our own businesses. We all worked through the calculations for several minutes in silence, until one girl put her pencil down and said, 'So you're telling me that I have to charge £2,400 for this plastic bangle? Nobody's going to pay that!'

If this is how you are feeling about your pricing right now, consider the following options.

COMPARE IT WITH THE MARKET: MAYBE IT'S NOT TOO HIGH AFTER ALL

Remember, just because a piece seems expensive to you, doesn't mean it is expensive in the context of the market in which it will be sold. Your spending habits are not necessarily representative of those of your potential customers, so don't let your personal reaction govern your prices too heavily.

Refer to the section on market research on pages 21–3. If you haven't done so already, do some market research. Try to find pieces of jewellery comparable to yours in terms of perceived value. What kinds of prices are they selling for?

Also, consult the section on branding, starting on page 93. The right branding can add tremendous value to your work, enabling it to be sold for much higher prices.

HAVE ANOTHER LOOK AT YOUR NUMBERS

A lot of calculations have gone into pricing your work. One small adjustment to any of these figures could have a significant effect on your prices. Go through the worksheets in this chapter and see if there are areas where you could make adjustments which would result in bringing your prices down. For example:

YOUR ANNUAL OVERHEADS: Lowering any of your overheads will result in a lower hourly rate. The difference between paying rent on a workshop and working from home will have a significant impact on your overheads and therefore your prices. Go through this worksheet and make sure you have been prudent with your outgoings.

YOUR ANNUAL PROFITABLE MAKING HOURS: Have you given yourself too much holiday time? Could you increase your weekly making hours to bring your hourly rate down? Avoid the temptation to simply increase the percentage in box F (the percentage of your stock that will sell) unless you have good reason to.

PRICING A PIECE OF JEWELLERY: The one number here that you can really play with is in box D – profit. I suggested trying 40 per cent, but if this isn't working for you, you may need to bring it down. The beauty of this system is that, so long as you have a positive number in box D, you are in theory making a profit (unless some unexpected cost arises which eats up your profit – which is why you shouldn't choose a figure lower than 15 per cent). Also, you don't need to put the same profit on every piece. It's good to try to stick to one figure for consistency's sake, but some particularly labour-intensive pieces may not be able to withstand the same profit margins as other, simpler ones.

CONSIDER MORE EFFICIENT MANUFACTURING METHODS

If it is the labour that makes up the bulk of your costs, you may want to think about other ways of producing this piece. If it is a one-off, would it be more efficient to produce it in quantity? Could you employ production methods to make it less labour intensive? For example, if you are piercing all your sheet metal by hand, could you have it stamped or laser cut instead? How would the costs compare?

CONSIDER LESS EXPENSIVE MATERIALS

This may seem obvious but it is easy to forget that you have options in terms of materials. If you are working in gold, would you consider gold plated silver instead? Have you researched your suppliers thoroughly? Are you getting your materials at the best possible prices?

CONSIDER MORE EXPENSIVE MATERIALS

Often the answer to too-high prices is to make the piece even more precious and more expensive.

Say, for example, you've made an extremely labour-intensive necklace out of sterling silver. For argument's sake, let's say you've done your sums and, because of the great number of hours, arrived at a retail price of £1,000. This seems a bit high to you, so you do your market research and find that comparable silver necklaces are selling for somewhere between £200 and £300. Yours appears rather steep in comparison.

Assuming that you can't feasibly make the necklace any quicker, you are stuck with a high labour cost which you just can't get around. But what would happen if you were to make the necklace out of gold instead? Your material costs would rise dramatically. So dramatically, in fact, that your labour costs would seem almost insignificant in comparison.

Let's say that the same piece, made in 18 carat gold, came to a retail price of £5,000. And let's assume that in your market research you saw other, comparable necklaces in 18 carat gold selling for around £8,000. This makes your necklace appear inexpensive. Although it is five times the price of your silver necklace, it is seen as better value.

A teacher of mine once said to me, 'Always use the most expensive materials that you can afford', and this example illustrates just why these are such wise words.

WHAT TO DO IF YOUR PRICES SEEM TOO LOW

If you've priced up a piece using the worksheets in this chapter, only to find that your retail price is lower than you'd expected, congratulations! Go to box D in the 'Pricing a Piece of Jewellery' worksheet on page 36 and increase the amount of profit until you arrive at a reasonable price.

But what is reasonable? This is answered through market research. Try to gauge the market as best you can, and price your work accordingly.

Also compare prices within your collection, and make sure they relate well to each other. For example, you wouldn't want a pair of silver earrings to retail for more than a similar pair of gold earrings. It's a good idea to make as many comparisons as you can think of within your own collection, making sure that your pricing 'makes sense'.

Wholesale vs retail pricing

What's the difference?

Wholesale refers to the price at which you sell your goods to shops, galleries and other resellers which buy from you in bulk to then sell to consumers. The key indicator of a wholesale transaction is that the goods are being bought for resale purposes.

The retail price is what you charge to an individual who is buying your jewellery for their personal use. In a retail transaction, the buyer is the end user. They may be buying for themselves or as a gift, but not for resale. As discussed earlier, the retail price will usually be about double or triple the wholesale price.

Most jewellery designers will deal in both kinds of transactions. Typically, you will sell some of your work to shops who will then add their mark-up and sell it retail. You will probably also sell your work at fairs which are attended by the public, where you will act as a mini-shop yourself, selling individual pieces to consumers at retail prices.

Tax

Make sure you understand your legal obligations in terms of tax. Depending on where you are based, you may need to tax wholesale and retail sales differently. In the UK, for example, if you are VAT registered, you must charge VAT on all of your sales, whether wholesale or retail. In the US, tax laws vary from state to state, and you may need to apply tax differently depending on whether a transaction is wholesale or retail. Refer to your government website (page 147) for further information.

Do I have to charge retail prices to the public?

Yes, you do. If, like most jewellers, you sell to both shops and to the public, please take note: do not undercut your stockists. It is tempting to entice people to buy from you directly by offering a discount, thereby 'cutting out the middleman'. Although this may indeed win you a sale, it is likely to damage your business in the long run. Take, for instance, the following cautionary tale.

Imagine that the owner of a gift shop meets Joe Greenhorn, a new jewellery designer, at an open studio event and buys twenty pieces from him. She displays his collection in the window, including a necklace which she bought at £50 wholesale and which is now priced at £150 retail. A young woman walks in, tries the necklace on, then disappears, having taken note of the designer. The customer looks up Joe and approaches him directly, saying how much she loves the necklace she saw in the shop, and could he perhaps do her a deal if she dealt directly with him?

Great, thinks the short-sighted young designer – an easy sale. I didn't have to pay for a stand at a show or do any advertising, and this customer has just landed on my doorstep! He sells her an identical necklace for £75. That way, he's still selling it above wholesale, so feels he's making a bit extra, and of course she's getting the piece for half of what it was in the shop, so she's thrilled. Everyone appears to be a winner.

The person who has lost out is the shopkeeper. She's put the time, effort and money into bringing Joe's work to the public, only to be betrayed. She may not find out, but news in the jewellery world travels fast, and designers who conduct themselves unethically soon get a reputation. Obviously, if Joe is found out he is unlikely to get another order from that particular shop.

But there is another factor to consider. The shop will only place a second order with Joe if his work sells well. The longer it takes to sell, the longer Joe will have to wait for the next order. If the work doesn't move quickly, the second order might never come. It is in Joe's interest to encourage shop sales.

Let's look at what Joe has gained by this: he has taken £75. He has also effortlessly acquired a new private client who may buy from him again in future.

And what has he lost? First, he has lost the additional £75 that he could have charged the customer. (For all he knows, she might have been happy to pay the £150 if he'd stood his ground.) Second, he has now set a precedent with the customer and will be expected to continue giving her big discounts should she buy from him again, possibly doing himself out of hundreds of pounds.

Even more unfortunate, he has also lost perhaps several years' worth of repeat orders from the shop.

Joe has earned himself a sale of £75, and a loss of perhaps thousands.

I repeat: do not undercut your stockists.

HONESTY IS THE BEST POLICY

The designer in this case has used the gift shop as a form of free advertising. That in itself is not necessarily a bad thing; if a customer approaches you directly, having seen your jewellery in a shop, you have every right to sell to them. But you must sell at a retail price.

Shopkeepers are trying to make a living, just like you, and most of them are reasonable people. They understand that you're not going to sell to your mother or best friend at retail. They will probably also understand if your advertised retail prices are slightly below theirs. Don't be afraid to have an open conversation with them on the subject. Remember, you are two cogs in the same engine, and the more you can work together, the better business will be for everyone.

Be honest with your retail customers, too. They should understand that you are obliged to adhere to certain business ethics and should not expect you to sell to them at silly prices.

MORE REASONS NOT TO SELL AT WHOLESALE PRICES TO THE PUBLIC

Apart from upsetting your stockists, there are greater reasons for not selling at cut-down prices to the public, ones that affect not just your business but the industry as a whole.

UNDERSELLING DEVALUES YOUR WORK

Have you ever seen a piece of jewellery in a shop and thought, 'I bet that costs a fortune!' only to look closer and find it's a fraction of what you thought it would be? How did you then feel about the piece? Did it seem less precious?

The value of a piece in the eyes of the customer is often down to what you tell them it's worth. If you say it's a £1,000 pair of earrings, they will 'ooh' and 'ahh'. If you say the same earrings are £30, you will get a different reaction. It's simple: if you put a low price on your work, your customers will accept it as being of a low value.

UNDERSELLING ATTRACTS THE WRONG CUSTOMERS

Who would you rather have as a loyal, repeat customer? The one who tries to beat you down on price, because she heard that you did a deal for a friend of hers? Or would you rather have a visit from the kind and considerate person who understands and appreciates the value of your work and is happy to pay the price that you ask? Each customer takes the same amount of your time; no doubt the latter will not only be more profitable to deal with, but more pleasant as well.

UNDERSELLING DEVALUES THE INDUSTRY AS A WHOLE

Just as supermarkets find themselves embattled in price wars which force everyone's prices down, reckless underpricing deflates not only your own profits but those of your peers.

I was exhibiting at a prestigious fair one year when word got around that one jeweller was selling handmade silver earrings for a mere £20. At this particular event it was unusual to see anything for under £100, so word spread fast and the designer was quickly identified. The design and craftsmanship of the earrings was superb; the designer's business sense was perhaps not. Judging from the amount of work involved, she was unlikely to be making any profit on them. Furthermore, she was making other makers' work appear expensive in comparison.

It is a free market and technically you can charge what you like, even if it means making a loss. But you're not only shooting yourself in the foot, you're crippling your fellow designers/makers too.

Commission-only jewellers

If you plan on working only to commission for private clients, then you may feel a little bewildered by this last section. You'll be pleased to know that the rules are a bit different for you, but that is only if you absolutely do not sell through shops or other resellers.

As I have explained at length, you must not undercut your stockists. However, if you work only to commission, and therefore have no stockists, you are not in danger of directly undercutting anyone. You will only have one price structure. Technically, your transactions fall into the retail category because your customers are end-users, but you will calculate your prices in the same way that other jewellers calculate their wholesale figures, with a few important differences.

Bear in mind that commissioned pieces tend to take longer to make. This is because each new design brief brings with it a new set of challenges. You may need to learn a new trick, find a new supplier or carry out various technical experiments to get the piece right. You will also need to spend more time with your client, as you will need to discuss designs and get approval at various stages. Because of the extra time involved in commissions, it makes sense to include design time in the pricing of each piece, rather than absorbing it into your overheads. You can do this in the following way:

1. First, in the section 'Determine your annual profitable making hours' on page 28, include design time in your 'making hours' instead of your 'admin hours'. Also include in your 'making hours' any time you think you might need to experiment, to find new suppliers, or any other research and development you may need to carry out in relation to specific commissions. In box F, enter a figure of 100 per cent, as you should expect to sell 100 per cent of the pieces that you make.
2. Then, when you come to price up an individual piece in the worksheet on page 36, include your design and research hours for that piece in the 'labour' box. You will charge all these hours at your hourly rate.
3. Go through the rest of the worksheet as explained, all the way down to box F. Although it says 'wholesale price' here, you can treat this as your retail price. Because you have included your design time, it should add up to a reasonable retail figure. You may also want to increase your profit margin in box D if you feel the piece can withstand it.

Finally, do not neglect the 'Troubleshooting pricing' section on page 37. This will largely apply to you too.

3 Selling your jewellery

Wholesaling: Selling to shops and galleries

One of the questions I am most often asked by jewellers just starting out is, 'How do you approach shops and galleries?' Most seem to be under the impression that there is a particular etiquette that they haven't been taught, a set way of doing things. 'Should I phone first, or should I email?' they ask. 'Should I send them some samples, or should I send pictures?'

Every retailer is different, so there is no strictly defined protocol. Whereas one shop may ignore all unsolicited emails, another may welcome them. Others might only order at trade fairs. Some galleries require applicants to fill in detailed forms, and may even request an interview.

The only way to find out how to get your work into a particular stockist is to ask them. There are, however, certain accepted routes which we will explore in this chapter. The most difficult part is the research and preparation that goes into finding the buyer and making the initial contact; after that, it's just a conversation, and how you proceed to the actual buying process is between the two of you.

Getting ready to sell wholesale

Successful selling is all about being prepared. Make sure the following are all in order before you embark on your sales campaign.

JEWELLERY COLLECTION

Be clear in your own mind about what you are offering, and be prepared to make this clear to your customers. For example, do you make unique, one-off pieces, or do you produce multiples? (Most shops will want to buy pieces they know they can reorder later. Galleries, however, will be happy to show your one-off pieces.) Do you have specifically defined and named collections? Can you alter lengths, colourways or materials if requested? (Turn to Chapter 4 for more about managing your collections.)

Do you offer branded packaging with your jewellery? Smaller shops will usually put your jewellery in their own shop-branded boxes, but larger retailers may ask you to provide your own. Be clear about what you offer and at what price. I sell my branded boxes to my stockists at cost if requested.

Website

One of the first questions you are likely to be asked when approaching a buyer is whether you have a website where they can view your work. It doesn't have to be complicated, but you need quality images that show your work at its best. (See Chapter 5: 'Your website'.)

Artist statement/curriculum vitae

Galleries will generally want to see an artist statement and curriculum vitae, whereas if you are more commercial you may have a brand statement instead. There are hundreds of online resources where you can find sample CVs.

An artist statement is just a one-page explanation of what your work is all about. For shops and galleries to sell your work effectively, they need as much background information about you as possible. Use this document as a chance to explain your inspiration, your vision and any unusual or interesting techniques you use.

Wholesale price list

You will need a wholesale price list, with photos, that you can send to potential buyers. This can be laid out however you wish, but it is normal for it to be on standard A4/letter-size paper which makes it easy to file. You should also have a PDF version ready to send as an email attachment, as this is a common request.

Order form

Although not always necessary, it is a good idea to have an order form for buyers to fill in by hand. You will probably only need this when dealing with a customer in person, for example at a trade fair, or if you visit their shop personally; otherwise orders tend to be placed by email or telephone. You'll need two copies, one for yourself and one for the customer, which can either be done the old-fashioned way with a piece of carbon paper, or by having your forms printed in carbonless duplicate pads. Be sure to include space on the form for the customer's billing and shipping addresses, which may be different. You should also include your terms and conditions, and details of how to pay.

TERMS AND CONDITIONS

Your terms and conditions are simply a statement of how you do business, and it is important that these are made clear from the outset. You can have these as a stand-alone document, or you may simply wish to include them on your wholesale price list so that buyers will have them to hand when placing an order. Ensure you have these in mind when dealing with buyers in person or on the phone, as they will certainly ask questions about how you operate. The following issues will need to be addressed.

MINIMUM ORDER

With wholesale orders it is standard practice to have a minimum order requirement – either a minimum value, or number of pieces, or both. This accomplishes two things:

First, it ensures that the order is in fact a legitimate wholesale order for resale, and not just a buyer taking advantage of his or her position. While it is perfectly normal for buyers to place small orders once they already carry a collection from you, it is also not uncommon for so-called buyers to approach designers at trade fairs to attempt to purchase single pieces at wholesale prices, with promises of exposure or future orders. A minimum order policy neatly circumvents this problem.

Second, a minimum order ensures that the retailer has a strong selection of your work on show. If you look in any jewellery shop window you'll see pieces grouped together by designer, or by collection. You wouldn't normally see just one or two pieces on their own: the display would be weak and ineffective, and wouldn't do the designer or the shop much good. Depending on your work, you might have a minimum order of, say, six pieces, or maybe twenty pieces if you feel that many are required to make a strong display.

PAYMENT TERMS

Your terms and conditions should state clearly if first orders are taken on a pro forma basis (in other words, with payment up front) and what the payment terms are thereafter. Pro forma invoices are explained on page 56.

Some designers also demand a deposit before they commence work on an order, typically around 50 per cent. Deposits are useful for two reasons. First, they can help fund the materials to make the order. Second, a deposit ensures the order is genuine; it is not unheard of for a buyer to place an order at a show, only to cancel it weeks later. If a non-refundable deposit is taken, the buyer is committed.

SHIPPING CHARGES

Many designers offer free delivery locally. Investigate the options available in your area, making sure your goods are insured while in transit, either by buying extra insurance from the shipping company or by ensuring you have a business insurance policy which covers this.

For international orders, and in many cases for national orders, shipping is a charge added to the invoice but which does not have to be quoted in precise terms at the time of ordering. Simply state that prices are quoted 'ex works' – in other words, exclusive of any delivery costs.

A list of shipping companies can be found on page 145.

DELIVERY TIME

Delivery time, or turnaround time, is something I personally prefer not to write into my terms and conditions. This gives me room for flexibility. When asked what my turnaround time is, I reply, 'When do you need it?' If the order isn't needed for three months, there is no point my rushing to finish it in six weeks just because that's the time that I've stated. Likewise, if an order is urgent but is actually quite small and manageable, I'll agree to do it quickly.

It is normal, however, to state a delivery time on your terms and conditions sheet; six to eight weeks is common.

Example terms and conditions:

Minimum order: £400

First orders are taken on a pro forma basis, 50 per cent deposit required

Standard invoice terms: Net 30 days

Prices are quoted ex works

Prices subject to VAT

TAX

Be clear about any taxes that will be added to your prices. If you are a VAT-registered maker in the UK, for example, you would state on your price lists 'All prices subject to VAT'.

Finding your wholesale customers

There are essentially two ways to get to your wholesale buyers: they can find you, or you can find them. Most designers will combine these approaches.

EXHIBITING AT TRADE FAIRS

When you exhibit at a trade fair, you are putting yourself in a position where retailers can find you easily. If it is an international fair, you will be exposing your business to thousands of potential buyers from all over the world. Most jewellers who deal in wholesale orders will attend several trade fairs per year, and it usually takes a bit of trial and error to find the most effective fairs for you. Because it is such a vast subject, an entire section has been dedicated to fairs, starting on page 63.

GETTING AN AGENT TO REPRESENT YOU

An agent will hold samples of your work and take orders from buyers on your behalf, either by exhibiting at trade fairs or by meeting with buyers individually. In return, they take a commission on all sales they make for you, typically 10–15 per cent. If you do go with an agent, make sure your wholesale prices can stand to lose this amount.

It is rare in the UK for a jewellery designer/maker to have an agent, but common in the US. When you are exhibiting at a trade fair you may be approached by agents. As with any business transaction, do not agree to anything immediately: do your research. Ask who else they represent and contact these people to find out more about working with the agent.

APPROACHING RETAILERS YOURSELF

Rather than waiting for the buyers to come and find you at a trade fair, there is always the option of contacting them yourself – yes, cold calling! Many designers find this approach a cheaper and more effective alternative to attending trade fairs.

COMPILE A LIST OF POTENTIAL STOCKISTS

Where do you see your work selling? Make a list of all the places you envisage stocking your work. Consider the following types of retailers:

GALLERIES: Contemporary jewellery galleries are now found throughout the world. They deal primarily in unique, handmade and innovative pieces, in both precious and non-precious materials. Jewellery is also showcased alongside other disciplines in craft galleries, and is often given space in galleries dealing primarily in fine art; in this setting, the jewellery may be exhibited in the same ways as the artworks, or it may be sold in a gift-oriented space within the gallery.

SHOPS: Jewellery shops are an obvious choice, but if your work is competitively priced it may also be worth looking at gift shops. Fashion boutiques will sell work by fashion-forward designers, and museum shops are always on the lookout for innovative products. Department stores are another option, and have the potential to place significant orders.

ONLINE RETAILERS: Online shops come in many formats, from specialized sites carrying work by a few select designers, to sophisticated commercial enterprises selling not only jewellery but everything from homewares to cosmetics.

DO YOUR RESEARCH

There will no doubt be dozens, if not hundreds, of potential retailers you don't yet know about, but these are easily researched. Find the website of a jewellery designer whose work is similar to yours in terms of style and price. Most designers include a list of stockists on their websites. These are your potential stockists; add them to your list.

Next, visit these stockists' websites and see what other jewellery designers they stock. Find those designers' websites and repeat the process of finding their stockists and adding them to your list. You will soon have a long list of potential wholesale customers. Some will be more appropriate for your style of work than others, so be sure to visit their websites – even better, their bricks-and-mortar shops – to get a feel for what they are all about.

PRIORITIZE

When approaching buyers, start with your first choice and work your way down. One very important factor is exclusivity.

Buyers often look for work which is not already being sold in their area, to maintain an advantage over their competitors. For this reason, they will sometimes ask you for exclusivity in their region. This could mean within a mile of their shop, or they might want exclusivity across their entire city, or even their county. So, imagine your distress when approached by your dream retailer wanting to place a huge order, with city-wide exclusivity, only to tell them that you already sell to the shop next door. You can avoid this kind of disappointment by approaching your preferred stockists first. Only when you have been rejected by them should you move on to your second choice. Not all buyers will want exclusivity, but it is something that will arise and which needs to be managed.

MAKE CONTACT

In theory, there are several ways you can make the initial contact with a buyer: in person, by email, by post, or with a telephone call.

I would not recommend dropping in personally, although it does work for some. Buyers are busy people, and it is unlikely that you will find one twiddling their thumbs waiting for you to walk through the door. An unsolicited visit is likely to be more annoying than anything, but if you like a challenge, you may want to try it.

Email is a less intrusive option – but for this reason it can easily be completely overlooked. If you are shy, you may find this suits you; however, an email on its own is unlikely to elicit a response.

With good, old-fashioned snail mail becoming ever rarer, your correspondence probably stands a better chance of being seen if it is sent by post. At least the envelope will be opened, unlike most unsolicited emails.

The best way to get through to a buyer, however, is to use the telephone. The idea of cold calling fills most designers with dread, which is exactly why you will stand out from the crowd if you do simply pick up the phone. Anyone can send an email; it's free and it's easy. But a phone call is up close and personal. Sure, you will have to deal with rejection head-on, but you'd have to deal with it anyway, regardless of your approach. At least if you've got someone on the phone, you've got their undivided attention – a difficult thing to come by.

Many of you will be well versed in conducting business over the phone, but for those of you who aren't, I've included some scripted ideas here. These are just guidelines, so use them as much or as little as you see fit.

Your first concern is finding out who the right person is to speak to: 'Hello, this is Jane Smith from Smith & Bloggs. I was wondering if you could give me the name of your jewellery buyer?'

Notice that you ask for the name of the buyer rather than asking just to be put through. This is important. Write down the name, and ask for the spelling if you need to.

Your second goal is to get that person on the phone: 'Thank you; could you put me through to him/her please?' If unavailable, find out when would be a good time to call back. If you do get put through, make sure you've reached the right person. ('Is that …?')

Then, you must clearly and succinctly state your business. Have something scripted so you don't stumble. You need to grab the person's attention and interest quickly: 'Hi, this is Jane Smith calling from Smith & Bloggs. We've just designed a new collection of jewellery made from ethically-sourced gold and vintage, rose-cut diamonds which I thought you might be interested in. I was wondering if it would be possible to make an appointment to show it to you?'

The answer could be anything from 'No thanks, and don't bother me again,' to 'That sounds really interesting! Could you come in first thing tomorrow?' If the response is positive, then give yourself a pat on the back, and make sure you follow up without delay. If the reply is not what you'd hoped for, don't worry. Move on to the next stockist on your list.

Dealing with sale-or-return

Jewellery is an industry of unwritten rules, and often the only way to learn is from experience. Decorum varies from country to country, and also within the jewellery industry itself, depending on the nature of your work and the retailers you deal with. One practice you are likely to come across is sale-or-return (S.O.R.), or consignment as it is known in the US.

Many shops, and especially galleries, will not simply buy your jewellery; rather, they will take it on a sale-or-return basis. This means that you deliver the stock to the gallery without any payment; the pieces still belong to you until they are sold, and only then are you paid. The retailer will normally issue you with a monthly sales report, and you may then need to provide an invoice for the goods sold. Sometimes no paperwork is required from you and the money will simply be transferred to your account.

The practice of S.O.R. is fairly peculiar to the jewellery world. It is most prevalent in contemporary jewellery galleries as opposed to more mainstream shops. If your jewellery is the sort of handmade, unique, highly individual work typically found in a gallery setting, you will undoubtedly be expected to provide work in this way, especially as a newcomer without much negotiating power. If, on the other hand, your products are more commercial and therefore easier to sell, you should seldom have to deal with this, especially if your price points are low.

PROS AND CONS OF SALE-OR-RETURN

The mention of S.O.R. is likely to elicit an exasperated rolling of the eyes from most jewellery designers. After all, life would be easier if we could all just get paid for our goods in thirty days like most people. As difficult as it is, however, S.O.R. does have some benefits and should not be dismissed out of hand. Consider the following:

PROS

FLEXIBILITY AND MARKET RESEARCH: Imagine that you produce a range of work and put it in a gallery on S.O.R., and it doesn't sell. What happens next? The gallery will probably give you some useful feedback as to why the work was unsuccessful and, based on that information, you may want to offer them a different collection, or adapt your existing one in response. With any luck you'll have more success the next time round. If you had sold that collection to a shop, and it hadn't sold, you'd have hit a dead end. They'd be stuck with stock they couldn't shift, and you'd have a hard time convincing them to buy from you again. With S.O.R., there is an ongoing conversation, a natural flow which is flexible and adaptable, and that could mean better sales for you in the long run.

PRESTIGE: It is usually the high-end galleries that insist on S.O.R., and having your work in a respected gallery can be valuable to your reputation. The fact that you have been selected to show there is enough to earn the respect of the jewellery connoisseur.

EXPOSURE: A gallery presence is also likely to lead to telephone calls from other retailers, who often scout for new and exciting work at such places. So, while the gallery may not buy from you, it may lead to other stockists who will.

CONS

CASH FLOW: This is by far the biggest problem created by S.O.R. If you are making work to fulfil an order, you know you'll be paid within (usually) thirty days of delivery. But with S.O.R., you might get paid in a few months, maybe a year, possibly never. It all depends on how long it takes for the pieces to sell. If you work in costly materials, you are not only delaying payment for your labour, but the money you've spent on gold and platinum.

STOCK ROTATION: Some galleries rotate the work they have on display. So while you sit in your workshop waiting for that sales report to come through, your work could be sitting in a drawer in the back of the gallery while another maker has a turn in the showcase. For this reason it is wise to try to stick to only doing S.O.R. with local galleries, so you can drop in occasionally and keep an eye on things.

Managing sale-or-return

Sale-or-return needs to be carefully managed; it is certainly a high-maintenance way to do business, and for this reason you must keep meticulous records and streamline your processes as much as possible. The following are a few administrative essentials that are unique to S.O.R.

SALE–OR–RETURN AGREEMENT

When you agree to embark on an S.O.R. relationship, it is essential that both parties sign an agreement. Not only will it protect you in the unfortunate event that something goes wrong, but it also makes clear at the outset what is expected from both parties. Some retailers will have their own agreement that they will ask you to sign. If not, you will need to provide your own. On page 136 is a sample agreement which you may use or adapt to suit you. Remember, these are only guidelines and an agreement is just that; it needs to be agreed by both parties. Present two copies to the gallery, both signed and dated by you. They should then sign and date both copies and return one of them. If they have issues with any of the points, this is the time to discuss amendments or altera-tions so that both parties are satisfied with the document.

DELIVERY NOTE

When you provide work on S.O.R., you must enclose a delivery note. This should be signed and returned to you as proof that the goods were safely received. Send two copies along with your delivery, one to be retained by the stockist and one to be returned to you. An example is shown on page 137.

STOCK MANAGEMENT

If you do a lot of S.O.R., you will need a streamlined stock management system to keep track of what you have on show and where. Whatever works for you is fine, but I'll share with you a simple system that I used successfully for years.

For each stockist, keep a file with all your delivery notes, arranged in chronological order. When you are notified that an item has been sold, write 'sold' next to it, along with the date and invoice number. Likewise, if stock is returned to you, write 'returned' and the date received. It is then easy to see, at a glance, what stock you have remaining with the gallery. If your delivery notes include pictures, all the better. This system also works well using a spreadsheet programme.

About once a year, typically at the end of the tax year, you should perform a stock check with all of your S.O.R. retailers. Put together a list of all the pieces that they still hold, according to your records. Send the list to them and ask them to check that their books tally with yours. If they do, that's great. If not, further investigation is required.

You also need to notify your stockists of any price increases. Just because you were wholesaling a piece for a certain price when you delivered it, it doesn't mean you are bound to this price forever. An occasional price increase, on a roughly annual basis, is absolutely fine. This is best run concurrently with a stock check. You can do this by adding an extra column to your stock check sheet headed 'new price'. Bear in mind that the gallery staff may not be able to enter the new prices into their system immediately, so a couple of weeks' grace period before changes take effect is normal.

Besides the practical aspects of S.O.R. stock management, you also need to keep a watchful eye on what is selling and what is not. If a collection is flying out of the showcases, replenish it! If a piece is displayed for several months without any interest, find out why, and discuss with the gallery the best way forward. It may be that it's just not right for their clientele; it may sell within its first week in a different location. The important thing is to have open and honest lines of communication with the gallery. After all, you both want the work to sell.

Invoicing and delivering orders

Whether you are working on S.O.R. or taking straightforward orders, you will have to raise invoices in order to get paid. (The exception is that some S.O.R. stockists will send you a monthly sales statement without needing an invoice from you.)

Generally speaking, the invoicing of a wholesale order can work in one of three ways. The first is where you provide the goods on S.O.R. and then invoice for pieces once they have sold. The second is where you take an order from a new customer and demand payment up front, via a pro forma invoice, which you then follow up with an actual invoice. The third is the most common once you've established a relationship with your customer: the customer places the order, and you deliver the goods and raise an invoice at the time of delivery.

PRO FORMA INVOICE

Most jewellers require first-time buyers to pay for goods in full before they are shipped. This money is billed with a pro forma invoice, a document which looks almost identical to an actual invoice except that it is headed 'Pro Forma Invoice' and may not have an invoice number.

The purpose of this document is twofold. First, it acts as a confirmation of the order, an agreement between you and the buyer. This is important, especially if the order was placed by telephone, or as a series of product codes scribbled onto the back of an envelope. The pro forma invoice will clear up any misunderstandings at the outset.

Second, it is used to obtain payment in advance. If you say to a buyer, 'First orders are on a pro forma basis', they should understand that this means they will need to pay up front.

The pro forma invoice is not to be confused with the 'real' invoice which is used for tax purposes. If you do obtain payment up front with a pro forma invoice, you will also need to raise a proper invoice once the money has been received.

A sample pro forma invoice can be found on page 140.

INVOICE

The actual invoice is what will be used for both parties' accounting records. Refer to page 139 for an example, along with detailed information about what must legally be shown.

In the normal run of events, for example with an established customer, you would simply send the invoice at the same time as you deliver the goods. If you are charging for shipping, you may want to wait until you know the exact shipping charges so you can invoice accurately. Send the invoice to the billing address as instructed by the customer; this will often be different to the shipping address.

If the order was carried out on a pro forma basis, in other words with payment being taken up front, then the actual invoice must follow as a legal requirement. It will also serve as acknowledgement that payment has been received. (Include the words 'Payment received with thanks' in place of your payment terms.)

DELIVERY NOTE

If you are delivering to an address other than the billing address, you will need to include a delivery note in the package. The easiest way to do this is to copy the invoice, change the heading and delete the payment information (see page 137 for an example of the invoice). Make sure the goods are clearly labelled so that they can be referenced to the delivery note; resealable plastic bags with code numbers written on them are sufficient.

Retailing: Selling to individuals

While many designers invest their time and money into breaking into the wholesale market, others take a more personal approach and concentrate on direct sales to individuals, in other words retail sales.

Getting ready to sell retail

A retail transaction is a more straightforward process than a wholesale one. You don't need to worry about terms and conditions, minimum orders or exclusivity deals. Whether selling at an exhibition, a market stall, over the phone or in your workshop, all that is really required to conduct a retail transaction is a way of accepting payment, a receipt book and some nice packaging.

TAKING PAYMENT

CASH

If you expect to be doing a lot of off-site cash transactions you will need a lockable cash box and a cash float. Keep a record of all your cash sales; as these tend to be for low-ticket items, the customer will often not ask for a receipt, so you must be sure to log your sales somewhere for your own records. A sheet of paper kept in the cash box should suffice. These sales can then be entered into your sales ledger on a regular basis (explained on page 121).

CHEQUE

The laws about cheques vary widely. In the UK, taking a cheque is now riskier than ever since the phasing out of cheque guarantee cards. In some countries – France, for example – it is a serious offence to write a bad cheque, so it rarely happens.

CREDIT AND DEBIT CARDS

Broadly speaking, if you plan on accepting credit and debit card transactions, you have two choices. The traditional route is to set up a merchant account, which is a particular kind of bank account where proceeds from card sales are held before being transferred into your business bank account. You then need to buy or hire a PDQ terminal (this stands for 'process data quickly') to run your card sales through, although you may be able to just process payments through an online portal, depending on your merchant account provider. Setting up a merchant account is a lengthy process, often taking several weeks, so don't leave this until just before a show.

The other option is to use a merchant aggregator such as PayPal or Square which allows you to take card payments without having a merchant account. Small businesses are increasingly turning towards aggregators, especially if they don't take a lot of card sales. The down side to this is that transaction fees tend to be significantly higher than for merchant accounts. You'll need to shop around and see which solution is the most cost effective for you based on your turnover.

At the time of writing, discounts on merchant accounts and credit card terminals are available to members of both the BJA (British Jewellers' Association) and the FSB (Federation of Small Businesses). It may be worth joining for these perks alone!

RECEIPTS

Not all customers will want a receipt, but you should have a receipt book for those who do. It needn't be anything fancy: a duplicate receipt book is fine. If you have the budget, you might consider having a custom receipt book printed.

PACKAGING

There are many companies specializing in jewellery packaging; a list is provided on pages 145–6. It is not essential to have custom packaging but it does add value to the jewellery, as well as reminding people of your name should they wish to buy from you again. You should also have bags of some description. Packaging can take anywhere from a few days to a few months to be printed, so investigate this well in advance of any shows.

Finding your retail customers

Finding retail customers is a subtler art than that of acquiring wholesale ones. Whereas there is nothing unusual about ringing up a shop to ask if they'd like to stock your product line, you can't really take this approach with individuals. You might market to them in a number of ways – advertising or social media, for example – but you can't just pick up the phone and start cold calling people. Instead, you need to put yourself in a position where your customers find you. There are several ways to do this.

EXHIBITING AT RETAIL FAIRS

When you exhibit at a retail fair, you put your work in front of people who are already interested in buying. They have, after all, made a special trip to the exhibition and have probably paid for a ticket. Although you will get a lot of students coming through, as well as people who just want a day out, this is also where you will find serious buyers. Again, see pages 63–71, where both trade and retail fairs are discussed at length.

MARKET STALLS

A relatively inexpensive way of reaching the public is by taking out a market stall, either as a one-off or on a regular basis. Although this won't suit all types of work, it can be a fun and profitable way to test the market without too much outlay. If you've never sold to the public before, it also gives you a chance to hone your selling skills, while testing new designs and gathering valuable customer feedback. Visit the street markets in your area. Look at the quality and price points of the work on show, and think about whether your work would fit in. One of the vendors should be able to point you in the direction of the organizers.

OPEN STUDIOS

If your studio space is part of an established group of workshops that hold open studio events, consider yourself very fortunate. This is a relatively effortless way of attracting retail customers, especially if the promotion and publicity are handled by an in-house marketing team. Such events are increasingly popular in major cities throughout the UK. Even if you are not a studio holder yourself, you may be able to participate in open studios by hiring out a vacant studio for the duration of the show.

A variation on the open studio theme is the idea of an open studio or open house 'trail' which might incorporate several open events under one banner. These are also becoming popular and might take place over one or two consecutive weekends. Often they showcase a combination of fine art, craft and design.

YOUR OWN SHOP

A shopfront ensures your work is available to buy all day, every day. Although it certainly deserves a mention here, it is a complex subject the scope of which is beyond that of this book. Running a jewellery business is one thing; running a shop is quite another, requiring additional skills and investment. If you are serious about opening a shop, buy a book on the subject and use the government websites listed on page 147 to obtain details of your legal obligations.

YOUR OWN ONLINE SHOP

A transactional website can be an inexpensive alternative to a traditional bricks-and-mortar shop. Refer to Chapter 5: Your website, starting on page 87.

NETWORKING

Networking is a more personal way to find retail customers. There are many different types of networking groups in operation all over the world, so you might want to investigate to see which suits you. Some are very business-focused, while others are more social. Either way, networking can be a great way to increase your visibility and build lasting relationships.

YOUR OWN EXHIBITIONS OR EVENTS

Once you start investigating retail fairs you will notice that it is an expensive business. With this in mind, it may be an idea to organize your own exhibition or retail event with fellow jewellers, or other artists or designers who might share a similar clientele to yours. It takes a lot of hard work to put on a show, much more than you might expect, so it is not something to be entered into lightly. Apart from all the usual preparations involved for a fair, you will also need to consider the following.

VENUE

You'll need to find a suitable location which is reasonably easy to get to. People are much more likely to pop into an exhibition if it's just round the corner from their workplace, or has easy parking or good public transport links. The venue could be anything from a gallery, to a restaurant, to your own home or workshop.

PUBLICITY

This is probably the biggest challenge you will face. Exhibition organizers have mailing lists stretching into the thousands; as a new business owner, you probably don't have this valuable resource. Gather names and email addresses of everyone you can think of who might be interested, or who might know somebody who is. Email them all. Print an eye-catching flyer and put it in as many places as you can. Design a window display for the venue, and organize some sort of signage for the duration of the exhibition to bring in passers-by. Send your newspapers and magazines a press release. Remember, nobody will know you're there if you don't tell them.

INVIGILATING

You basically have two options here: you can require all exhibitors to be present for the duration of the exhibition, or you can take it in turns to look after each other's work. With the latter option, you will need to draw up a rota and make sure that whoever is on duty is fully briefed on everybody's work so that they know how to sell it properly.

ACCEPTING PAYMENT

You will want to be able to take payment by card, probably with a mobile credit card terminal. If all exhibitors are to be present all the time, then each can simply organize their own method of taking payment, as with any other fair. If you choose the rota system, however, you will need a way of taking cards centrally. One option might be for all exhibitors to leave their terminals with whoever is on duty. Or, if you are showing in a gallery space, they may offer to take credit card sales on your behalf for a small fee.

Working to commission

Working to commission can be very satisfying. From a design point of view, making a piece to order will always present certain design and technical challenges. Plus, it's a more personal way of doing business, as you are likely to spend a lot of time with the client discussing and honing the design until it's just right. There is an important financial benefit to commissioned work as well. Unlike making work for stock, you can make the piece safe in the knowledge that your materials and labour are being paid for.

Some jewellers specialize in working to commission and are happy to create whatever the client wishes, no matter the style. Others might only take on work that is in keeping with the look and feel of their signature collection.

The first thing that happens with a commission is an initial consultation (normally free of charge) where you meet the client to discuss the details of the job, including design, materials, budget and deadline. You then come up with an idea, or a selection of ideas – depending on what you feel is appropriate and what the client has requested – as well as an estimated price. How you present your designs depends on your drawing skills and what is appropriate for the job. If you are creating a bespoke ring to a client's rough sketch, you might want to present a highly accurate CAD drawing to make sure you've interpreted the sketch correctly, and to iron out the details. Or, if the commission is based on a piece already in stock in the studio, you may simply be able to explain a concept using existing pieces as examples, with sketches to support your ideas. It all depends on how you work.

If significant gemstones are involved, it is standard practice to get a selection of stones on approval from your stone dealer for the client to choose from. If the design is based around the stone, this might be your first step, before producing any drawings. On the other hand, you might need to get the client to approve a design before you proceed to the stone selection process. There are no set rules.

For help with pricing, use the worksheets in the 'Pricing your jewellery' section starting on page 33, paying attention to the special notes on pages 43–4 for commission-only jewellers. You will want to present prices – estimates at least – along with your design concepts. If they are estimates as opposed to firm quotations, you must make this clear, in writing, so that there are no misunderstandings later on.

The client may not be happy with your initial designs, of course, and you might be asked to make changes or suggest alternatives. This is normal. Unfortunately, you can't really charge any extra for this, as it is all part of the design process; the client cannot be expected to pay more in the event that he or she is not satisfied with your first concept.

Once the design is approved, it is customary to ask for a 50 per cent payment up front. This ensures the client is committed to the process and should allow you to buy the materials without being out of pocket.

Then it only remains to make the piece. Be sure to give yourself a realistic deadline, especially if the design or construction is outside your usual comfort zone and there will be a learning curve. Keep your client updated with progress, as well as any deviations from the estimate, as soon as you become aware of them. Nobody likes nasty surprises, and you want the delivery of the piece to be a happy occasion. Make sure it is beautifully packaged and that your client leaves with a smile on their face.

Trade and retail fairs

What are they?

Fairs are exciting events where dozens or even hundreds of companies come together under one roof to sell their wares and promote their businesses. Each fair is different: it can be anything from a massive trade event with leading businesses from around the world taking part, to a homespun gathering at the local village hall. Generally speaking, however, there are two types of fairs: trade and retail.

TRADE FAIRS

At a trade fair (also called a trade show, trade exhibition or expo) you exhibit your jewellery and take wholesale orders from shops, department stores, galleries and other retailers. In other words, it's a B2B (business-to-business) event. You only need to have one sample of each design on your stand as buyers will place orders which you will deliver at a later date. At most trade fairs you will see a vast mix of exhibitors, from global brands to budding start-ups. You will also find manufacturers of jewellery tools and equipment, packaging, gemstones and other related items. For this reason, trade fairs are worth visiting even if you're not exhibiting, as they provide an unparalleled opportunity to keep up to date with what's going on in the trade.

RETAIL FAIRS

These are B2C (business-to-consumer) events, where you sell directly to the public at retail prices. These might be jewellery fairs, craft fairs or art fairs. Customers will generally take their purchases home with them, and special commissions might be placed as well. It is common to find trade buyers browsing at retail fairs too, so a reputable retail fair will often function unofficially as a trade fair as well, with wholesale orders being made and future exhibitions discussed.

How to exhibit at a fair

DO YOUR RESEARCH

Each fair has its own style and unique focus. You can think of fairs as being like shops: some just sell jewellery; some sell a broader range of goods such as home furnishings and gifts; others may only sell ethical products, or children's clothing and accessories. Visit as many fairs as possible and try to get a feel for where your work might fit in.

You need to find a fair where the quality and price points of other exhibitors' work is on a par with your own. Quality exhibitions attract quality buyers. You will benefit not only from the reputation of the event, but from the mailing lists of your fellow exhibitors, many of whom will have been trading for decades and will have invited hundreds of their customers – who just might become customers of yours.

On pages 142–3 you will find a list of trade fairs which cater either partially or exclusively to the jewellery trade. After visiting a few of their websites you will soon see how much variation there is. Visit as many shows as you can in order to determine where your jewellery would best fit in, and scour the internet for fairs in your local area.

BOOK YOUR STAND

The best spaces get snapped up first, so contact the fair organizers and book your stand as early as possible. It's not uncommon for larger fairs to take bookings a year in advance.

The big fairs often have sections dedicated to designer, handmade or limited-edition jewellery, so if this applies to you, make sure you are placed in the appropriate section. Discuss stand options with the organizer to find the space that best suits you. But remember, their job is to sell you a stand, and if no appropriate spaces are left, they might just try to sell you a space elsewhere. Do not allow yourself to be talked into taking a badly positioned stand.

TYPES OF SPACE
When dealing with major fairs, you will generally find there are two types of exhibition spaces available: space only or shell scheme.

SPACE ONLY
When you take a space-only stand, you are hiring just that – space. In other words, a block of air. Everything else needs to be bought or hired by you: carpet, walls, lighting, electricity, signage. Fortunately, it tends to be just the larger stands at the major fairs that are sold on a space-only basis, so you are unlikely to have to deal with this when just starting out.

SHELL SCHEME
Smaller spaces are often sold with a shell scheme, where you hire an area of floor space, plus the walls around you. You will almost certainly have to pay extra for lighting and electricity, which you do through the organizer. Some shell schemes, especially at smaller fairs, include extras such as showcases, lighting and perhaps even a chair. Each fair is different, so make sure you know exactly what's included in your basic stand fee.

PREPARE
Start preparing as early as possible. You've got a learning curve ahead of you, so leave time for things to go wrong.

PLAN YOUR STAND LAYOUT/DISPLAY
I find the best way to start planning is to find somewhere to mark out your floor space using masking tape. Stand in the space and get a feel for how it will function with you inside it. Bear in mind that at some fairs the stands are very shallow and you're not expected to stand in the space, but to linger next to it in the aisle. It is, however, more common to stand or sit in your space. Knowing

what is expected is just one more reason to visit a fair before you exhibit.

Think about what type of showcases will work best for you and your work. If you work in non-precious materials, you might even consider doing away with showcases and having your work displayed so that it can be picked up and tried on without the barrier of a locked cabinet. You will also need somewhere to store all of your paperwork – a small filing cabinet or a box file. You'll also need some sort of a surface to write orders and wrap people's purchases on. (Low, horizontal showcases can double up as desks.) You'll also need a space to hide your personal belongings, preferably with a lock. Display cabinets often come with lockable storage space underneath.

Make use of wall space by displaying images or other information about your work. The organizer should advise you as to whether you will be able to paint your walls, and whether the use of nails or screws is allowed. Make sure you know this before you plan your layout. If nails and screws are forbidden, you can usually still hang images and shelves using large hooks over the top edges.

How you display your jewellery within your stand is an art in itself. Experiment with different types of props. Make sure you know the exact dimensions of your cabinets and mock up your displays at home or in your workshop. Take photos of them and use these for reference on set-up day. It will save you hours of valuable time.

PRICES – DISPLAYED OR HIDDEN?

The culture of price display varies from fair to fair. Sometimes it is absolutely expected that you show prices with your work. However, there are some fairs where nobody divulges prices without being asked. The only way to know what's expected is to visit the fair before you exhibit.

In certain situations it makes sense to keep prices hidden. For instance, if you are at a trade fair with wholesale prices on display, you risk those prices being seen by members of the public who invariably get in. One solution is to attach tiny tags with code numbers to the pieces. You then need one price list for retail customers, and one for trade buyers.

BUY/HIRE SHOWCASES AND FURNITURE

Major exhibition companies will have preferred showcase hire companies for you to use, but many people prefer to buy their own. Hiring saves a lot of hassle as the cabinet will be delivered direct to your stand and removed at the end of the fair.

ORDER LIGHTING AND ELECTRICITY

In terms of lighting and electricity, find out from the organizer what is included in the cost of the stand and make sure you order yours in plenty of time. There is normally a fixed charge per electricity socket. Lighting often comes in the form of spotlights attached to the back of your stand's fascia. A cost-saving way around the price of spotlight hire is to just order the electricity and bring your own halogen lights. Remember, you might also need electricity for other things including your computer, phone charger or credit card machine. You may also have to prove that all of your electrical goods have been PAT (Portable Appliance Testing) tested by a qualified person.

ORGANIZE TRANSPORT

If you are providing your own showcases or other furniture, you will need to organize a van for set-up and set-down days. If you are hiring your display cabinets, you might be able to get away with putting everything you need into a giant suitcase.

ORGANIZE INSURANCE

You will not only need to insure the jewellery, but you will need public liability insurance as well, to safeguard against the unfortunate event that a member of the public is injured while peering over one of your showcases. Make sure your business insurance policy includes public liability insurance.

PLAN AND MAKE YOUR STOCK

Possibly the most daunting task involved in preparing for a fair is that of stock planning. How much stock do you need, and how do you plan for it?

Trade fairs are relatively simple. You only need one of each piece to show, as buyers will be placing orders, not taking work away immediately. If you mainly create one-off pieces, that's fine too – obviously you will only have one of each anyway.

With retail fairs it's a bit of a guessing game. You could just have one of each piece, and when it's gone, it's gone. Or you could make multiples of everything in the hope that your work sells like hot cakes. Alternatively, you could do something in between, maybe making multiples of your predicted bestsellers. The tricky thing of course is that if this is your first fair, you don't know what people are going to buy. There is one way around this: show one of each design, and take orders at the show – similar to what you would do at a trade fair. This carries the risk of losing sales, especially of lower priced, impulse purchases. For major pieces, however, customers are usually very understanding, and will sometimes thoughtfully suggest the idea themselves.

Forgetting for a moment how many multiples you'll need of each design, you need to think about how many different designs you need on show to make a good display. The number will vary depending on the nature of your work.

Like a valuable oil painting, an exquisite piece of jewellery needs a frame – in other words, space around it. This lends an importance to the work, drawing the eye to the piece and allowing it to rest there. For this reason, you can be sparse with expensive or otherwise important work. It should make a statement.

On the other hand, if your stock in trade is silver ear studs, you can imagine how lost they would look if given the same treatment. To be seen in the first place you will need a decent quantity of them. Consider the size of the cabinet and what quantity will make a strong display.

When you've decided how much stock you need and what you plan to make, use the time management tools described on pages 109–14 to help devise a production schedule. Don't forget to leave plenty of time for hallmarking, especially at busy periods such as the run-up to Christmas.

ORDER YOUR PACKAGING

If you are planning for a retail event, make sure you order your boxes and bags well in advance.

PUBLICIZE THE EVENT

By participating in a well-known exhibition you benefit immensely from the attendance of regular visitors who show up year after year. However, you should take it upon yourself to publicize the exhibition as best you can. Don't just rely on the mailing lists of the organizers or other exhibitors; even if someone has been invited by another designer, they still won't have a personalized invitation to your stand.

Send invitations out to as many potential buyers as you see fit. Whether you do this by email or post is up to you; personally, I do both just to be sure all bases are covered.

If you are lucky enough to have some private clients already, invite them to all of your retail events. At the least, invite friends and family. They are likely to be your first clients, and will act as fantastic ambassadors for your business.

Invite the press to all your events as well, and include a press release with your invitations; information about how to write one can be found on pages 103–4.

PACK

Now that you've carefully prepared everything you need for the event, it remains only to pack it all up and take it to the fair. A sample packing list is shown below. This is similar to the checklist I use myself and, although you will want to amend it to suit your needs, it should trigger a few ideas.

FURNITURE AND ACCESSORIES

- Plinths/showcases/cabinets
- Trolley (for moving showcases)
- Chair
- Shelves
- Showcase keys
- Glass cleaner/cloth

JEWELLERY PROPS/DISPLAY

- Coloured paper for display
- Craft knife
- Price tags
- Blu-tack
- Business card holder
- Postcard holder
- Flower vases

WALLS

- Paint, brush, roller
- Signage/photos/press cuttings
- String or cord
- S-hooks (to go over walls)
- Spirit level
- Measuring tape
- Hook-and-loop tape
- Nails and screws
- Hammer

- Screwdrivers
- Thumbtacks
- Ladder

ELECTRICAL

- Extension leads
- Fuses
- Light fittings
- Spare light bulbs
- Electrical screwdriver
- Electrical tape

STATIONERY AND ADMIN

- Price lists
- Order book
- Receipt book
- Business cards
- Postcards
- Notebook
- Mailing list book
- CV/artist statement
- Press releases
- Stapler
- Scissors
- Pens and pencils
- Calculator
- Tape
- Mobile phone
- Mobile credit card terminal and charger

OFFICIAL FAIR PAPERWORK

- Exhibitor badge
- Vehicle pass

JEWELLERY AND RELATED ITEMS

- Jewellery(!)
- Orders for collection
- Silver cleaner
- Surgical spirit and cotton wool (to clean tried-on earrings)
- Mirror
- Ring sizer
- Ruler
- Packaging – boxes and bags

Exhibit!

Once at the show, relax. If you've done your preparation, the hard work is now behind you. If you don't have any selling experience, don't worry – just be yourself. Your enthusiasm for your work will sell it for you.

AT THE EXHIBITION

Wear your own work (if appropriate). Most jewellery looks better on than in a case, so make sure you attract attention by showing it off.

Get the work out of the cabinets at every opportunity. If somebody asks about a piece, even casually, take it out of the case to show them – don't wait to be asked. This will not only give the customer a chance to engage more closely with the piece, but will also attract attention from passers-by. For the same reason, you should chat to as many people as possible – even students who you know are not going to buy. A crowd attracts a crowd.

Rearrange your display if you think it's not working. Any cabinet will have certain 'hot spots' that somehow attract the eye. Plus, it is a well-known phenomenon that rearranging a tired display often results in a flurry of sales. The act itself of redisplaying attracts sales as well, as customers will feel more comfortable approaching you if you've already got your hands in the cabinet.

Stay positive. A happy and relaxed standholder is infinitely more approachable than one with a face like thunder. If things aren't going well and you're feeling grumpy, take a break. Get somebody to mind your stand for half an hour so you can take your mind off things for a while.

Treat everybody equally. Don't judge prospective customers by their appearance: wealthy people do not always look and dress the way you might expect. Plus, just because somebody can't afford your work now doesn't mean they can't engage with your work and become a fan – and fans are an invaluable source of free publicity.

Protecting your designs

When you make your work available for sale, whether at a fair, through a shop or online, you are throwing your designs out there to the public, and there is nothing to stop the less scrupulous members of society from copying your designs and profiting from them. It may or may not happen to you, but it is a real risk – which is why you should at least be aware of the dangers, as well as the steps you can take to protect yourself.

I asked Nigel Jackson, a solicitor with a wealth of experience in this area, to write a few words on the subject. Below is a synopsis of the current legislation and how it applies to jewellery designers.

Design protection... a legal note

As jewellery designers and manufacturers, there may be designs which are of particular importance to your business and which are sufficiently important that you wish to protect them.

The law on design protection within the UK and Europe is complex and, to put it mildly, is a bit of a 'legal maze', given that designs can be protected on an unregistered design basis, or even to a limited extent by copyright. The other way to protect them, however, is by formal registration of a design at the IPO (Intellectual Property Office) in the UK or at the OHIM (Office for Harmonization in the Internal Market (Trade Marks and Designs)) in Europe.

As markets become more complicated, and the need for distinguishing your products from the opposition becomes paramount, it is likely that more copyright and design infringement actions will take place round the world. It is therefore worthwhile taking time to consider whether or not you should protect your work by carrying out design protection either within the UK or Europe, or on a worldwide basis.

Design registration

Registration of designs is not that expensive and has the advantage of effectively giving you a monopoly for your design for a limited period. Such registrations are being carried out by a number of eminent jewellers and fashion designers round the world.

But the protection obtained is worthwhile for even a small jewellery business as it effectively protects your products from infringements and makes it much easier to sue for infringement or piracy. To get an idea of design protection, look on the IPO website, www.ipo.gov.uk, at the sections on design registration.

Also look at the EUIPO website which protects intellectual property throughout Europe: euipo.europa.eu/ohimportal/en. These sites will give you an idea of what is involved and the approximate costs of design registration.

Does your design qualify?

Working out which elements of your design may be suitable for this form of protection can be a complex issue. Aspects which are purely functional, such as the chain on a necklace, or the clasp fittings, may not be suitable for design protection as they may be considered to be functional parts of the design. However, the overall design of a piece of jewellery, subject to it being unique and not like other items already being sold or protected within the marketplace, may well be appropriate for design protection. If you think it may be necessary for your work, it is best to seek legal advice. The costs of design registration are not prohibitive and are well worth it, especially if you are considering trading your jewellery throughout the UK, across Europe and worldwide. Such registrations will also enhance the value of your business and, in due course, can enable you to get a much higher price for your business or your company if you decide to sell it.

4 Managing your stock

Your collections – general considerations

Before getting into the finer points of stock management, it is worth taking a look at the different approaches designers take to structuring their collections. In the context of this chapter, the term 'collection' refers to a specific group of pieces which hang together and which are meant to be either worn together or displayed as a group. Collections often have names that convey the idea behind them – the Geo collection, the Sunburst collection, the Petal collection and so on.

A question that often comes up is 'How many pieces should go into a collection?' There is no simple answer to this. The best way to judge for yourself is to do your market research (see 'Conducting market research' on page 21) and notice how collections are presented in the retail environment. A collection could comprise, say, as few as four designs – a necklace, a bracelet, a pair of earrings and a ring. (With so few pieces, these would each have to be very impactful.) You could also have a collection of only bracelets, or only earrings – possibly hundreds of them. The important thing is that you have a strong theme running throughout which ties the pieces together. You might even have a collection within a collection – it is completely up to you.

Some jewellers will bring out a new collection twice a year (fashion jewellers particularly) or perhaps annually (often in the run-up to the winter selling season or an important fair). Some will add and remove designs from an existing collection over the course of several years. This approach often means treating certain items as 'core' pieces – those which remain constant over time – and 'seasonal' pieces which are introduced for shorter periods.

One-of-a-kinds vs multiples

Some jewellers only produce unique items (in other words, once it's gone, it's gone). These are commonly referred to as 'one-off' pieces in the UK and 'one-of-a-kind' or 'custom design' pieces in the US. Quite often the decision to work in this way is driven by the jeweller's choice of materials and methods; for example, found objects may be featured or techniques with unpredictable results may be employed. In the case of the artist jeweller, to produce the same design twice might be unthinkable. Many choose to work on a one-of-a-kind basis because they simply find the idea of making something a second or third time too tedious.

Other makers favour the efficiency and even the repetitive nature of producing multiples of the same design. There are several advantages to working in this way. Many pieces can be generated from a single design, a clear time saving over designing each and every piece individually. Multiples also lend themselves to batch production techniques, popular examples being casting and laser cutting. And because of these time and cost savings, multiples generally have lower costs than comparable one-offs. Customers are, however, likely to expect such pieces to be priced correspondingly, so this must be borne in mind.

One advantage to working in multiples is that work can potentially be outsourced or 'farmed out' to a manufacturer, or even to another maker or workshop. This opens up a whole new world of possibilities in terms of capacity, pricing and target audience. If you wish to explore outsourcing, a good place to start is by visiting manufacturers' stands at some of the larger trade fairs.

Rings

Rings deserve a special mention here because of the sizing issue. They are inherently problematic because, unlike most necklaces, earrings and so on, they have to fit perfectly. When fabricating a ring, there is always the question of what size to make it. When you think about it, it's actually highly unlikely that the person who walks into the shop and wants to buy a particular design will just happen to have the right size finger for the one on display.

If a ring is a one-of-a-kind, this can be particularly problematic. Essentially, you have three choices. First, you can choose not to alter the ring, thereby losing the sale. (However, if you are lucky the customer will select another ring from your collection!) Another option is to resize the ring for the customer, if the design allows for this. Finally, you could remake the ring. However, it would then no longer be a one-of-a-kind, so you would not want to do this if the piece had been marketed as being unique, unless you destroyed the original. A way around this is to advertise such a piece as a 'limited edition' rather than a one-of-a-kind. Because you've removed that promise of uniqueness, you are now free to remake the ring, either in a different size or perhaps with slightly different stones or some other minor change.

If the ring is a multiple, the sizing issue is much easier to deal with. If a wholesale buyer places an order which includes several different ring designs, it is a good idea to provide each ring in a different size. That way, if a customer likes your style of work (but is not committed to one particular design), they will have several pieces to choose from. The more common scenario is for the customer to simply choose the ring design they want and place an order for the correct size.

Your stock management system

Your choice of stock management system will depend on the factors discussed above, as well as the extent of your inventory and whether you work on a S.O.R. basis. Every jeweller I know has a different system for keeping track of their stock; there is no right or wrong way. Whatever your method, however, you will need a way of recording at the very least a description, price and date sold for each piece. How you do this, and what additional information you choose to include, is up to you.

The old-fashioned way: Keep it in writing

There is nothing wrong with keeping a handwritten ledger of all of your stock, especially when you're just starting out. If your inventory consists of tens of pieces rather than hundreds, you may find that this works for you. (I even know of a long-standing gallery which kept track of all of its stock in this way right up into the twenty-first century, with great success!)

The comprehensive solution: Stock management software

There are several digital stock management systems on the market and your decision whether to go this route – and if so, which package to choose – will depend largely on the level of sophistication you require. One of the main benefits of commercially available systems is that they typically integrate your invoicing with your stock management, so that your stock levels are automatically adjusted each time you raise an invoice. Most systems on the market are far beyond the needs (or the means) of the average designer/maker, but there are two that I have personally used with success. KashFlow (www.kashflow. com) is online accounting software for small businesses which includes stock management functionality. The other system is inFlow (www.inflowinventory.com), which is a comprehensive inventory management system from which you can also generate your invoices and a range of useful, customizable reports. These products and others on the market are constantly evolving, so be sure to do your research and sign up for a free trial before committing to anything.

The halfway house: Spreadsheet software

If you prefer the analytical power of a digital system but feel daunted by choosing and getting to grips with a dedicated piece of software, you may find Microsoft Excel (or other spreadsheet programme) perfectly sufficient for your needs. Once you have your information in spreadsheet format, it is easy to extract information using the 'filter' tool and perform multiple calculations (such as price increases) automatically using basic formulas.

When setting up your inventory spreadsheet, consider which of the column headers below might be useful:

- *Name and/or description*
- *Serial number and/or model number* – If you produce unique pieces it is a good idea to give each one its own unique serial number. If you produce multiples, you will probably want to assign a number to each design rather than to each individual piece. You could also combine the two systems so that each multiple is assigned a model number (indicating the design) as well as a unique identifier.
- *Collection* – The name of the collection that the piece belongs to, if any.
- *Type of piece* – Necklace, bracelet, brooch, ring, etc.
- *Materials*
- *Dimensions* – You will be asked for this information whenever submitting photographs to the media or to exhibition organizers.
- *Weight* – This is always a useful figure, particularly if you are working in precious materials.
- *Location* – If the piece is on S.O.R. in a gallery you will want to know where.
- *Retail price*
- *Wholesale price*

- *Prices in other currencies* – If you regularly sell abroad you may wish to standardize your prices in other popular currencies to make ordering easier for your buyers (bearing in mind you will have to suffer any losses resulting from adverse foreign exchange movements).
- *Unit cost* – If your work is manufactured, record the unit cost.
- *Time to make* – Some makers record this information as it can be useful for planning future work flows, or for pricing up new pieces.
- *Date added to inventory* – This information will be useful later when you need to determine the value of your stock on a given date (for accounting purposes).
- *Invoice details* – Invoice number, date, amount and the date the invoice was paid.
- *Name of buyer*
- *Quantity in stock* – This will only apply if you create work in multiples and choose to record them all as one line item rather than separately with their own serial numbers.

In deciding which of the above to include, bear in mind that in Excel you can filter by multiple columns. For example, you could filter by 'Collection' and by 'Location' to see which pieces from a certain collection you had in stock at a particular gallery. The 'Sort' tool works in a similar way, and allows you to sort your spreadsheet based on the values of any number of columns.

Once you learn the basics of your spreadsheet software, you will be able to do things like:

- filter to see who your best customers are;
- extract information to give to your accountant to complete your tax return such as your sales for the year, or the value of your inventory (see below);
- automatically adjust prices to reflect annual price increases or a change in the price of precious metals;
- generate wholesale and retail price lists in different currencies;
- identify sales during a certain time span or from a particular stockist.

If you haven't yet discovered the ways in which spreadsheet software can help you in your business, I highly recommend going on a short course or reading *Excel for Dummies*! Be warned, however – spreadsheets are addictive!

Valuing your stock for accounting purposes

Your accountant should be able to advise how to put a value on your stock for the purpose of your annual accounts. As a general rule, inventory should be valued at the lower of a) cost or b) net realizable value. In other words, you should value it at what it cost to make, unless it has become apparent that you will never be able to sell it unless you do so at a loss, in which case its value is what you expect to get for it! You will need to provide your accountant with the value of your stock as of the last day of each tax year.

Inventory and cash flow

One of the big challenges that makers face, especially those working in precious materials, is how much inventory to hold. This is especially difficult if you work on a S.O.R. basis because you will have to produce enough work to provide a decent display to each gallery, as well as a healthy supply of pieces to top them up as their displays thin out. However, having too much stock has serious drawbacks. Once you've spent your money on the materials to produce all that work, the money is stuck there (in other words, it is 'illiquid') – you can't extract it and use it to pay for a trade fair stand, or a new computer, or your next month's rent. (Well, in theory, perhaps you could if you were working in precious materials – in which case you could melt your stock down in times of crisis!) In other words, by having high levels of stock you are depriving your business of cash that could be used for other things. Quite simply, it is a cash flow issue.

Think of it this way: your inventory is a money-making machine. How expensive you choose to make this machine is up to you. As you will see in the next few pages, the most expensive machine is not necessarily the most efficient or profitable one.

An efficient and profitable inventory is one that 'turns over' as quickly as possible. While we all know this in theory (it is obviously better to sell work quickly), most jewellers don't put much effort into ensuring that their stock is 'working hard' for them. For this reason I would like to illustrate just how crucial this concept is with an example. (This is deliberately oversimplified for demonstration purposes, so please bear with me!)

Let's say you just have one necklace design that you make over and over again. You sell it through a gallery, Gallery A, which (rather unusually) is happy to have just the one piece of yours in their window. As soon as the necklace sells, you instantly take your earnings, fabricate the piece again, and supply it to the gallery. (For the purpose of this illustration we are going to imagine this all happens in an instant.) The materials needed to make one of these necklaces come to £200. This means that, at any given time, you've got £200 tied up in that piece. Obviously it's not the same £200 – you keep 'recycling' this investment each time you sell and then remake the piece. By 'recycling' I mean that when you are paid for the necklace, you take £200 of your winnings to make the next necklace, keeping the remainder as profit.

For the sake of argument let's say your wholesale price for this necklace is £500. As the materials cost you £200 this gives you a gross profit of £300. Gallery A sells this piece, on average, once per year. This means you make a gross profit of £300 per annum on your £200 investment.

Say you have an identical arrangement with another gallery, Gallery B. Gallery B's customers are particularly taken with this piece, so much so that it is sold (and immediately restocked by you) once a month – twelve times per year. At £300 gross profit per piece, this earns you £3,600 per annum, *all from that initial £200 investment.* You only had to fork out the £200 for materials for the very first necklace; when you received the £500 from the first sale, you took £200 of that and spent it on materials for the next piece and took the remaining £300 as profit. Although individual pieces of stock may come and go, that £200 remains invested.

If you had £200 to invest in materials, would you rather it earned you £300 with Gallery A or £3,600 with Gallery B?

Although this is an oversimplification of how things work in real life, it illustrates the importance of the *speed* at which your stock turns over. When your work moves quickly, it means your inventory is 'working harder' for you. This is why it is useful to identify which distribution channels (i.e. galleries) sell your work the fastest – especially if you work on a S.O.R. basis, where your cash is tied up in the stock that you provide to them.

How to identify your fastest selling S.O.R. stockists

This section is aimed at jewellers who regularly work on a S.O.R. basis because it is they who really have to keep an eye on their stock to make sure it's moving quickly.

It is easy to identify which stockists sell the highest *volume* of work – all you have to do is look at your sales figures. But are these your bestselling stockists simply because you've given them loads of stock (a sizeable investment on your part) or is it because they move the stock that they do have quickly? This takes a bit more effort to identify, but it is not impossible. There is a well-known formula for calculating this.

INVENTORY DAYS

This is a formula for calculating how many days your stock takes, on average, to sell – or to 'turn over'. In this context, we are going to be using it to identify your speed of turnover on a per-stockist basis. (It can also be applied to your entire inventory, or perhaps to a certain region, etc.) By using this formula, you will identify the number of days, on average, a piece of your work takes to sell in a particular retailer. You will need to have been working with this particular shop or gallery for about a year if you are to get an accurate reading.

The first step is to calculate the average wholesale value of your work in that retailer during the course of a given year. You could do this by picking a high and low level from the course of the year and averaging these out. For a more accurate reading, you could pick several points throughout the year and take an average of these. We will call this figure your 'average inventory value'.

The next step is to simply add up your sales from that shop or gallery for the year. Again, you are working on a wholesale basis so be sure to use your wholesale price (i.e. the amount you received). Ideally you want the sales which actually occurred during the year in question, regardless of when you were paid for them. We will call this figure 'annual sales'.

Next, divide your average inventory value by your annual sales and then multiply this number by 365. The result is the number of days it takes, on average, for a piece of yours to sell in this gallery.

Inventory Days – the formula

$$\frac{\text{Average inventory value}}{\text{Annual sales}} \times 365$$

To show how this works in practice, let's look at the examples of Gallery A and Gallery B. For both galleries, the average inventory value is easy to work out. In each case, you had the one necklace stocked on a constant basis so the average inventory value would be £500 (the wholesale price).

For Gallery A, the piece was sold just once during the year, so annual wholesale sales were £500. Let's plug the Gallery A figures into the formula:

$$\frac{\text{Average inventory value of £500}}{\text{Annual sales of £500}} = 1. \text{ Multiplied by } 365 = 365 \text{ days.}$$

This means it takes 365 days – one year – for a piece of stock to sell at Gallery A (which we already knew)!

Now, to prove the formula works, let's apply the same logic to Gallery B. The average inventory value is £500. The necklace sold 12 times during the year so your annual sales on a wholesale basis were 12 x £500 = £6,000. Here's how those numbers work in the formula:

$$\frac{\text{Average inventory value of £500}}{\text{Annual sales of £6,000}} = 0.0833. \text{ Multiplied by } 365 = 30.4 \text{ days.}$$

As you can see, the Inventory Days formula has told us what we already knew about our turnover rate at Gallery A and Gallery B. I hope this illustrates for you that the formula works. What is much more exciting is to apply it to your own S.O.R. galleries to see how they compare. Once you have identified the high-speed conveyor belts that take your work from display to sale quickly, you will know that these are the stockists you should probably be giving more work to.

INVENTORY TURNOVER RATE

Another way of looking at how quickly your inventory moves is to ask yourself how many times your stock turns over during the year. The formula for this is sort of an inverted version of what we've just done.

Inventory Turnover Rate – the formula

$$\frac{\text{Annual sales}}{\text{Average inventory value}}$$

For Gallery A this works out as follows:

$$\frac{\text{Annual sales of £500}}{\text{Average inventory value of £500}} = 1.$$

In other words, your inventory turned over once during the year.
Likewise, for Gallery B:

$$\frac{\text{Annual sales of £6,000}}{\text{Average inventory value of £500}} = 12.$$

As you can see, your stock turned over 12 times during the year.

PUTTING THE FORMULAS TO USE

Hopefully I've proven to you that these formulas work. Let's now
apply them to a more realistic situation. Say you have work on
S.O.R. with a third gallery, Gallery C. Gallery C has a range of your
designs in stock with an average inventory value of £4,000. Your
sales for the year came to £6,000. This gives you an Inventory
Days figure of £4,000/£6,000 x 365 = 243.3 days, and an Inventory
Turnover Rate of £6,000/£4,000 = 1.5. Your sales from Gallery C are
identical to those from Gallery B, but not because they move the
work quickly. With each piece taking an average of 243.3 days to
sell, the only way to get good sales from Gallery C is to give them
loads of work, which is an expensive way to operate!

The performance of each gallery is summarized below.

	Gallery A	Gallery B	Gallery C
Average inventory value	£500	£500	£4,000
Annual sales	£500	£6,000	£6,000
Inventory Days	365 days	30.4 days	243.3 days
Inventory Turnover Rate	1 time per year	12 times per year	1.5 times per year

Now that you know how to identify who sells your work the
fastest, the next question is what to do with this information. Say
you have a range of work in the above three galleries and come
up with the turnover figures above. Galleries A and C are clearly
lagging behind Gallery B, but what does this mean for you? What
action should you take?

For starters, you might want to have a conversation with
Galleries A and C to ascertain why your work is turning over so
slowly. Is it that your designs are just not right for their clientele?
Are the prices too high (or too low) for their customers? Is the
work being displayed badly (or worse – being kept in a drawer
in the back room)? It may be that you just need to try different
collections at Galleries A and C that are more suited to their
customer base – just because one collection didn't work doesn't

mean you won't be more successful with another one. These things are difficult to predict and a bit of experimentation is often required.

You may ultimately decide that you want to take your work out of Galleries A and C and put it all into Gallery B where it will sell like hotcakes. But before you rush into this, consider the following factors which may diminish the effects of this move:

1. Market saturation: Gallery B only has so many customers. It may be that the amount of stock you provide to Gallery B is exactly enough to satisfy their customers' demand for your work. In other words, it could be that the market for your work at that gallery is already saturated. If this is the case, the addition of more stock will not lead to an increase in sales.

2. Display: Gallery B might not be willing or able to display more of your work than it already does. Or it may be that they already display one of each of your designs, meaning that, were you to supply more stock it would only be duplicates of what they already have, which would be kept in their back room until your display needs restocking. Therefore, supplying them with more work might not have any effect.

3. Reputation/Publicity: It could be that, although Galleries A and C are slow to sell your work, they are having a positive impact on your sales elsewhere. They might be proactive in promoting your work through exhibitions or in the media, but just not very good at selling it – perhaps because their mark-ups are too high or because they have incon- venient opening hours. In other words, having your work in Galleries A and C could indirectly be supporting your sales at Gallery B.

4. Diversification of risk: Having your work in a variety of stockists has the effect of reducing the risk of poor sales. If you rely too heavily on one gallery, you will be in trouble if they go bust or even if they have a bad season due to factors beyond your control. (We will take a closer look at diversification in Chapter 8.)

5. Past performance is not necessarily a guide to future perfor- mance! Remember, you can never really predict future sales with any certainty.

Stock management, especially in the fickle and volatile world of jewellery design, is a bit of a black art and something that you will ultimately get a feel for through trial and error. Hopefully the ideas presented in this chapter will help provide you with the tools to analyse your current situation objectively and to manage your stock (and your cash flow) better in future.

5 Your website

What is it for?

A website is no longer a luxury; it is now an essential component of any serious business. This is not to say that you need to have a sophisticated online shop, or even anything more than a single page. The complexity and depth of your site should be dependent on what you want it to accomplish.

Who is your audience?

Who do you hope to reach with your website? Are you hoping to use it to attract private clients, or will it serve more as a brochure for wholesale customers? Will you use it to keep the press up to date with your latest news? Think about all the different audiences you hope to speak to through your website. Look at other jewellers' sites for inspiration.

What do you want it to do?

A website can have many functions. First and foremost, it is a communication tool and a great platform for building your brand using words, pictures, sound and video. In this respect, it has all but obliterated the role of the company brochure. As we all know, however, a website does much more than just inform; its potential applications are almost limitless.

The biggest question you will face when launching a site is whether you want to sell online. The decision to build a transactional website is not something to be taken lightly, as it adds extra cost, time and responsibility, all of which are explained here.

Another major consideration is whether you want to be able to easily update your site yourself. If so, you will probably be looking at building a CMS, or content management system, into it.

Design and build

Given the time and inclination, you can design and build your website yourself. However, if you are serious about your online presence, and if you can afford it, you might be better off hiring an expert. I would suggest hiring an expert, especially if you want to sell online, which complicates things immensely.

The technicalities of building a site are changing all the time, so I won't go into too much detail here. Whatever the current technology, though, there will be varying degrees to which you can become personally involved in the process.

Design and build it yourself

In the infancy of the internet, building a website meant learning HTML code. Nowadays, not only do you not need to be a coder, you don't even need to be a designer. There are dozens of online web builder tools on the market, and new ones are coming out all the time. Most of these offer free or low-cost templates for you to use and adapt to reflect your brand, many with e-commerce capabilities. If you are just starting out and have the time and inclination, you could do worse than build your website yourself using a platform such as Wix, Godaddy, Moonfruit or the numerous others available. Many designers also use selling platforms such as Etsy either in substitution for or in addition to their own website.

Hire an expert

If you are serious about your online presence and you feel your time would be better used tending to other areas of your business (such as making jewellery), you may be better off hiring a website designer. You will probably get a better result and your sanity just may remain intact. When choosing a designer, try to get a referral from a friend or colleague; there is no better way to ensure you are hiring somebody competent and trustworthy.

Briefing a designer

To get good results, the designer needs a detailed brief. Make a list of what you need the website to do. If you want to update it yourself, be specific about which parts (products, news, events, etc.), to make sure they are all included in the CMS. Define your target audience: wholesale or retail, or both. Does your work appeal to a specific demographic? How computer literate is your audience? The more of this kind of information you include in your briefing, the more direction your designer has, the more likely he or she will come up with a successful result.

Do not forget the crucial subject of maintenance and support. Who will fix your site in the event that it crashes or gets hacked into? If you hire an individual rather than a company, what happens if your site goes down when they are on holiday? Things will go wrong occasionally – that's just the way it is – make sure you know how this will be handled, and what costs are involved.

SHARING THE WORKLOAD

You may also choose to come up with the general design of the site yourself, and have a technically competent person build the site based on your drawings. If you are on a tight budget but are not technically minded, this might be the option for you. A website designer will probably not be keen on working this way; however, a web developer, in other words someone who specializes in the technical side of building a site, will usually be quite happy to be directed.

Selling online

YOUR RESPONSIBILITIES

Regardless of how you go about building your online shop (should you choose to go the e-commerce route), be aware that as an online seller you will have certain legal responsibilities. You will also have responsibilities to your customers who will (rightly) expect a certain level of service.

CONSUMER CONTRACTS REGULATIONS

Whether you are selling through a website or via mail order, there are distance selling laws to which you must adhere. In the UK, these are set out in the Consumer Contracts Regulations which are summarized on the UK government website at www.gov.uk/online-and-distance-selling-for-businesses. The key points to bear in mind are that you need to a) make clear your business details, b) give consumers certain information about your products, including their right to cancel, and c) give customers a 'cooling off period' within which they can return the goods. Check the small business pages of your government's website (see page 147) to see what your legal obligations are.

TIMELY SHIPPING

On your site you must be clear about how long a customer can expect to wait for an item to be delivered. You could just have a generic statement saying that all pieces are made to order and therefore take a certain amount of time to ship. Alternatively, you could have a stock control facility built into your site whereby in-stock items show up as shipping within 24 hours, and out-of-stock items as shipping in four weeks. It's up to you, but it's something that deserves careful thought, as you will be tied to any promises you make. You may wish to restrict the countries you are willing to sell and ship to, to avoid the complications associated with exporting such as tax, customs and variable reliability of local delivery services.

PRICE UPDATES

The prices on your website will need to be kept up to date. You'll probably want to put all your prices up once a year or so, either by inputting the information yourself or having someone else do it for you. Changes in tax rates also need to be applied as and when they occur.

FRAUD

Online purchases are cardholder not present (CNP) transactions which by their nature are highly susceptible to fraud. Unfortunately, if you accept a CNP payment made using stolen credit card details, you are likely to be held responsible, even if your bank authorizes the transaction. This may seem unfair but that's the way it is – by agreeing to accept payment without the cardholder standing in front of you, you put yourself into a very vulnerable position. When setting up your merchant account or signing up with a merchant aggregator service, be sure to make yourself aware of these risks and how you can mitigate them.

Selling offline

There is a way around the complications of online selling which might save you a lot of time and money – that is, if you are willing to forego the convenience and prestige that comes with having a transactional online shop. You could design the site in such a way that instead of buying online, the customer is instructed to email or call you to arrange payment. This may lose you a few impulse-buy customers, but if you're just starting out and you're on a budget, it might be the answer.

Even if you have a transactional website, you may find that

some customers prefer to buy in person or over the phone. They might use the website as a research tool, a way of browsing without any pressure or obligation, and then give you a call once they've got an idea of what they want. I'd say that my website generates as many sales of this type as it does online purchases.

If you specialize in bespoke pieces, then this approach would make perfect sense. Use your website to showcase your work and what you're capable of. Invite customers to contact you, perhaps via a form on your contact page, to discuss their commission ideas in detail.

Drive traffic to your site

No matter how amazing your site is, nobody is going to find it unless you tell them it's there, especially in the crowded jewellery market, where global companies with marketing budgets in the millions can bully your site into oblivion. Try typing 'jewellery' into a search engine and see which companies appear at the top of the list. Narrowing it down to 'designer jewellery' or 'contemporary jewellery' may yield more interesting results, but you can still see how busy the market is.

Creativity is important not just in the design of your website, but in driving traffic to it. You could hire a professional, perhaps the person who built your site, to optimize it to increase traffic. This is called search engine optimization (SEO). It can be expensive but it works. The big jewellery companies all use SEO experts – that's one reason they come up first in search engine results. You can investigate this route if you wish, or you can do a few things yourself which are either free or inexpensive.

Google Adwords

Presumably you've noticed that, in Google search results, there are usually a few highlighted links at the top and on the right-hand side of the page. These are paid for with Google Adwords. Investigate further by visiting adwords.google.com.

Email marketing

Building an email list can be difficult in the beginning, as you are unlikely to have many clients to market to. Start with your friends and family, and encourage them to forward your emails to their contacts.

Do not even think about buying lists of email addresses. The rest of the world hates junk mail just as much as you do. Instead, collect relevant email addresses at every opportunity. At exhibitions, have a mailing list book. Better yet, have some sort of prize draw which encourages potential customers to give you their email addresses. Be careful that you do this legally, however. Currently customers need to opt in (in other words, to tick a box) to allow you to send them information by email.

If you want to create professional-looking newsletters, complete with clickable links to your website, have a look at mailchimp.com or constantcontact.com. They both have loads of useful tools for creating and tracking email marketing campaigns – a great way to drive traffic to your site.

Finally, in every email you send, include a link to your website in your signature. Encourage people to click through by occasionally including a link to an event page or new product, along with a clickable picture.

PR

In the PR section, starting on page 99, you will find a wealth of ideas for spreading the word about your business. Make use of these avenues, both analogue and digital, to alert the public to your website and drive business to it.

6 Presentation is everything

Branding: Being clear about your business

'But I'm just a small business!' you cry. 'I'm not a brand!'

Whether you like it or not, if you are in business, your business has a brand. If you haven't devised a brand yourself, then the public will have created one for you. This is because branding is not just about logos and slogans; branding is how the public perceives your business. So, if you've just done your first exhibition, you've already sent a message to the public explaining what you're all about. In what sort of venue was it? Who else was exhibiting? What were your price points? How did you speak to your customers? Whatever your answers, the people who encountered your stand will have come to their own conclusions about you and your business. They might think you are expensive, cheap, cutting edge, traditional, agreeable, difficult, mysterious, down-to-earth...

Think of it this way: your business is a living thing. Like a person, it has a personality. In business, this personality is called a brand. And just as your own personality influences the way you dress, speak and behave, so your brand pervades everything that you make, say or do.

Presumably, you would like your jewellery, and therefore your business, to be perceived a certain way. If your work is made for going out clubbing in, then you will want to project a different image to, say, a brand specializing in fine gem-set jewellery. Branding is about making sure this is clear, by stating in no uncertain terms what your values are as a designer and as a business. This clarity is vital to your business for two reasons.

The first one is trust. Your customers need to be reassured that you are a serious business, not some fly-by-night operation that's going to be forgotten in a few years' time. If you present yourself coherently and professionally, you will establish yourself in your customer's mind as a business worth dealing with.

Second, when somebody makes a purchase from you, they are making a statement about themselves – their tastes, their aspirations, their values. If your brand values are clearly aligned with those of your customer, you help your customer to make this statement about themselves by buying from you. They shouldn't be aware of the fact that you are saying, 'Hey, my values and your values are the same, so buy from me!' It is much subtler than that.

Identifying your brand values

Take some time to think about what you, as a business, stand for. What is your jewellery all about? What words do you use to describe it? How would you like others to describe it? Is it fun, serious, young, sophisticated, dark, light...? List all the characteristics you can. Don't just talk about the physical attributes of your jewellery; think about the emotions and feelings it might convey – words such as relaxed, aggressive or quiet. Universal words like these are especially useful in building a brand because of their potential breadth. Once you've settled on a concept or a few key words, the branding comes easily. It's just a matter of keeping your brand identity in mind at all times.

Applying your brand to your business

Remember, your brand is the personality of your business, and should shine through wherever possible. This means making sure that all your communications, actions and decisions are in line with your branding. This includes:

PRICE POINTS: Your prices have a huge effect on how your work is perceived. If you are targeting a wealthy audience, you won't be doing yourself any favours by underpricing your work to the point where it is perceived as cheap.

PHOTOGRAPHY: Your product shots should be as clean and straightforward as possible, but when shooting work on a model (lifestyle shots) you will really have a chance to reflect your brand values.

WEBSITE: This is another fantastic opportunity to clarify your values using words, photography, animations and sound.

BLOG: What you choose to blog about speaks volumes about your brand, as do your tone of voice and writing style.

NEWSLETTER: The same goes for your newsletter, if you have one.

STUDIO LOCATION: Whether part of an artistic residential neighbourhood or in a swanky, commercial end of town, your studio location says much about your company.

CHOICE OF FAIRS AND STOCKISTS: Being seen in the 'right' places does wonders for your reputation. Make sure they are right for your work and your brand.

SPEAKING VOICE: Do you address your customers formally or more casually? Do you project businesslike confidence, chirpy charm, or are you calm and collected?

PERSONAL PRESENTATION: Convey your values through what you wear and how you present yourself. Treat your appearance as another extension of your creativity.

Visual presentation

PHOTOGRAPHY

As a jewellery designer or jewellery artist, it is relatively easy to build and promote a memorable visual identity for yourself because what you do is, by its very nature, visual. Think of a designer whose work you admire. What image springs to mind? My guess is that it's an image of their work. Your jewellery is the bedrock of your visual identity.

Excellent photographs are crucial, as they will get you into exhibitions, win you awards and will get printed in magazines. Poor photographs, on the other hand, will get you nowhere. It is worth investing in professional photographs of your work. Photographing jewellery presents all sorts of technical difficulties because it is small and often reflective. For this reason alone you should look for a photographer who specializes in jewellery, and make sure you see samples of their work before agreeing to anything.

PRODUCT SHOTS

Product shots, or packshots, are the bedrock of your photo library. This type of shot has one aim: to show the work at its best. To achieve this, shoot everything on a white background. The images will be clearer and also more attractive to magazines, which often need 'cut outs' – shots with a totally white background, so that no border appears around them. (Look at the 'shopping' pages of any glossy magazine for examples.) Some exhibition organizers will even insist that you submit images on a white background with your application as it allows them to compare entries more easily.

DO—IT—YOURSELF PRODUCT SHOTS

Depending on the nature of your work and your photographic skills, you may be able to get away with taking your own packshots, thereby saving a small fortune. (Do remember, however, that good photography is worth its weight in gold; do not settle for substandard pictures.) Be prepared for a lot of trial and error.

EQUIPMENT

If you are going to shoot your own images, you will need a few essential pieces of kit:

DIGITAL CAMERA/SMARTPHONE: Whatever you use, it will need a macro setting, and preferably a timer setting to avoid camera judder. Take a piece of your work into a camera or phone shop and test out a few models to see what works best for you.

TRIPOD: This is essential to avoid blurring. A cheap one should be perfectly adequate. You can get tiny tabletop tripods that are perfect for this sort of work.

LIGHT TENT: Whether you need this will depend on the nature of your work. It is basically a box made of a colour-neutral fabric which acts as a light diffuser, thus eliminating any harsh shadows. Tents can be bought from online sellers or camera shops.

LIGHTS: Ideally you should have two lights, although you may only need one. These must be fitted with daylight bulbs to achieve accurate colour. Again, these are readily available online, or from camera shops.

IMAGE EDITING SOFTWARE: Most people use Adobe Photoshop for retouching, but look around for cheaper alternatives. Some editing is always necessary, if only to ensure a totally white background.

METHOD

On a tabletop, set up your light tent (if you are using one) with the open side as close to the edge of the table as possible. Arrange the jewellery on the floor of the tent, or on a piece of white paper or acrylic sheet. Place either one lamp overhead, shining down onto the work, or if you are using two lamps, arrange one lamp on either side. Experiment with light angles for the best effect.

Mount the camera on the tripod and get it as close as possible to the subject. Make sure you have selected the highest possible image quality on your camera. Use the macro function, and make sure that the colour setting is switched to daylight. Because the image will be mainly white, the camera will want to darken the overall picture to bring it down to what is considered average brightness. Increase the brightness setting to counteract this. It will take some trial and error to get this setting right.

Finally, get the piece in focus, and use the timer setting to take the shot. This eliminates the risk of camera judder and ensures the clearest possible picture.

Upload a few images to your computer before spending hours shooting all your work, as you will need to tweak your lighting and camera settings to get them just right. Use your image editing software to make any necessary colour adjustments and to ensure the background is flawless and white. Crop the image as required.

LIFESTYLE SHOTS

When jewellery is photographed on a model it is generally referred to as a 'lifestyle shot'. This kind of image is used to create a certain atmosphere or mood, to suggest a concept beyond the jewellery itself. This is a much more complex task than a straight product shot, and will require not only a model but a hair and make-up artist at the bare minimum; you are likely to also need a stylist and possibly someone to art direct the shoot for you. It is quite an undertaking and best left in expert hands. Rest assured, however, you don't need this sort of photography when you're just starting out. Spend your money on good product shots instead.

LOGO AND STATIONERY

For most businesses, the logo is the core of their brand identity. Although as a jewellery designer your product photography is likely to be your most powerful visual asset, a strong graphic identity is still important, as it unifies and therefore strengthens all of your printed and online marketing material.

Why is this important? For a start, a strong, relevant visual identity inspires trust in your company, and trust is crucial to making sales.

There is an advertising term known as the 'rule of seven'. It has often been said that someone has to see an advertisement seven times before they act on it. Forget the exact number – the point here is that people need to see your logo/product/company several times before coming round to the idea of buying from you. Only once you feel familiar to them will they take that step forwards. To breed familiarity, everything you ever print or publish needs a distinctive look and feel. The more consistent your visuals, the more familiar they will feel to the viewer, and the more likely they will be to buy from you.

A strong visual identity also adds value to your products. Which will be perceived as more valuable, a silver necklace in a plain plastic box, or that same silver necklace carefully wrapped and presented in custom-made packaging complete with your embossed logo and matching ribbon?

LOGO OR LOGOTYPE

Whereas a logo is a symbol or illustration of some sort, a logotype (or wordmark) consists of only your company name, drawn or set in a unique and distinctive way. As a new jewellery business, a logo is not necessary but you do at least need a logotype. This will appear on your business cards, packaging, website and wherever possible in print and online.

Ideally you'll want this professionally designed, but the truth is, jewellery start-ups can rarely afford this. If you take the do-it-yourself route, you would be wise to follow the tips below.

DO-IT-YOURSELF LOGOTYPE

Spend some time experimenting with different typefaces and colours until you find a solution that conveys the correct mood. Every typeface has its own personality, its own voice. Choose yours wisely. Once you decide on a particular font and style in which you write your company name, stick to it. Consistency is key.

You should also choose a supporting typeface that you consistently use on printed material. This could be the same as your logotype font, perhaps in a different weight. If you choose a different typeface, just follow this one simple rule: if your logo uses a serif font, use a sans serif for your supporting typeface. And vice versa. Two serif fonts together will clash, as will two sans serif ones.

Your wordmark should be placed in the same way throughout your marketing collateral. For example, always centered, or always in the upper right-hand corner.

PRINTED STATIONERY

Your visual identity will need to be applied to your printed stationery, which will include some or all of the following:

BUSINESS CARDS: These are essential and should be carried with you at all times. Many designers put a product shot on the reverse side; this is a great way to instantly explain what you do, but if you bring out a new collection every six months then an image will shorten the business card's useable life. Consider small runs of digitally printed cards if you want to change the image often.

LETTERHEAD: It used to be essential to have printed letterhead (with matching envelopes, continuation sheets and complements slips), but these days it is perfectly acceptable to just set up a template in your word processing programme and use it to create all your correspondence.

POSTCARDS: Most makers have postcards to hand out at exhibitions, with a photograph of their work on one side and contact details on the other. These are also useful if you need to handwrite a quick note to enclose in a package. It's a good idea to get new postcards printed once or twice a year and enclose them with exhibition invitations and other correspondence. There are companies which specialize in artist postcards; a list can be found on page 146.

PACKAGING: Depending on your work, you will probably need a few sizes of box for different kinds of jewellery. There are specialist jewellery packaging companies which will print your logotype on the boxes for you; see pages 145–6 for a list of suppliers.

PR: Managing your reputation

Branding and PR are inextricably linked. While branding is about creating an image and an awareness of your business, PR (public relations) is about managing your reputation. It's all about nurturing the public perception of your business.

Although many companies owe their successes to the sheer magnitude of their PR campaigns, it is something that can quickly burn a hole in the pocket of the small start-up business. On the whole, jewellers start out doing it themselves.

Most people think of PR in terms of getting seen in the press, but it doesn't stop there. It's about making sure that everyone knows how wonderful you are. This means not only the press, but also your customers, your colleagues, your staff (if you have any) and your entire network of contacts. The goal is to keep your company in the forefront of everybody's minds and for the right reasons. The following pages aim to explain just how to do this.

Do interesting things

One way to get noticed is to do interesting things. As a creative person, you do this anyway; you are (I hope) constantly coming up with new designs or taking on exciting commissions. Noteworthy activities might include:

NEW COLLECTIONS: Every time you bring out a new collection, or create a magnificent one-off piece, you've done something newsworthy, so keep those new collections coming.

WINNING COMPETITIONS: Enter as many competitions as you can, as winning them will not only give you PR fodder but will earn you publicity through the competition organizers, who will promote your winning design on your behalf.

COLLABORATIONS: Do you have a friend working in another discipline who you can collaborate with? Could you work with a fashion designer to create some pieces for a new collection? Do you know a painter, sculptor or architect who you could bounce a few ideas around with? Perhaps you could team up with another jeweller with complementary skills to create a unique piece showcasing both of your talents. Be on the lookout for collaborative opportunities; they usually result in interesting work and extra publicity.

ORGANIZING AN EVENT: Do you have an idea for an unusual event in which your jewellery could play a part? Could you organize a special exhibition, charity fundraiser or competition?

Tell everyone about it

Doing interesting things isn't going to do your reputation much good if you don't shout about it. Inform everyone, including:

THE MEDIA: Magazines, newspapers, newsletters, relevant websites – news is their lifeblood and you need to provide it by supplying them with a press release. (More about this on the following pages.)

EXISTING CUSTOMERS (WHOLESALE AND RETAIL): Customers like to be loyal but you need to make it easy for them by getting in touch occasionally, and a news story is the perfect excuse. It not only reminds them that you exist, but it makes you sound interesting and boosts your reputation.

POTENTIAL CUSTOMERS: Beware of spamming laws, which vary from country to country. If you have permission from a member of the public to send them details of news and events, then you can safely do so, as long as you give them the opportunity to unsubscribe from your list. Building up your status in the eyes of your potential customers is a great way to encourage them to make that leap and buy from you.

FRIENDS AND FAMILY: Don't forget, friends and family can become customers too. Add these to your 'potential customers' list; even if you don't think they will ever buy from you they might forward your news to people who will.

COLLEAGUES: It's good to keep your fellow jewellers, university lecturers and outworkers posted with your activities. It pays to keep yourself in the limelight within your industry as it generates respect from your peers and may lead the way to unexpected opportunities.

SUPPLIERS: Informing your suppliers of what you're up to is another way to strengthen your reputation within the industry. If you are seen to be a rising star, your suppliers may be more willing to bend the rules and help you out with rush jobs or other tricky requests.

ALERT THE MEDIA WITH A PRESS RELEASE

Writing your first press release can be daunting, simply because you don't know what is expected and what format it should take. It is, however, a pretty straightforward process.

Say you have a news story (a new collection, an exhibition, a collaboration, for example) and you want it to be featured in a certain magazine. You simply need to compose a one-page document, called a press release, with details of your news, and at least one eye-catching photo. This can be sent by post or by email, but I would recommend calling the recipient first to give them a quick explanation over the phone, and to ask which delivery method they would prefer. This phone call accomplishes several things. It gets their attention, so when your press release comes through it is not completely new to them. It also checks whether they are the most appropriate person to send the release to. (They may refer you to a different department instead.) It also establishes what format they would prefer to receive the story in, and gives you a chance to check that you have their correct email or postal address.

WHO TO SEND YOUR PRESS RELEASES TO

Keeping a database of press contacts is an ongoing job. Journalists rarely stay at one publication for long, so you'll find your carefully-researched contact list in a state of constant flux. You've got to start somewhere, though, so the first thing to do is to visit your local news-stand or library, where you can pick up every magazine you wish to target, and make notes of the relevant contact names.

Towards the front of any magazine you will find a list of the editorial staff. If it's a glossy fashion magazine, make a note of the jewellery editor. If there is no jewellery editor, your next port of call should be the fashion editor. As you can imagine, the fashion editor of a national glossy is going to be extremely busy, with press releases coming at them left, right and centre. So, while you will definitely want to send them something, you might have more luck with the shopping editor, the person who looks after the 'shopping' pages where various products are gathered together along a particular theme.

Another place to look for names is on the editorial pages of a magazine. Find an article that has some relevance to you. The writer may be credited in the introduction to, or at the end of, an article. Or their name may be tucked into the spine of the page – flatten the magazine out and you should find the name hidden in the spine.

If you are approaching a broader publication such as a national newspaper, you are unlikely to find a jewellery editor. They may have fashion editors, or it may be the arts editor that you contact. You just need to find the person most closely related to the subject that you are writing about. Don't restrict yourself to jewellery and fashion-based publications. If you've got a new collection based on plant life, there's no reason you shouldn't send it to a gardening magazine. (You might have to tailor your press release to suit.)

HOW TO WRITE A PRESS RELEASE

Before you start writing, think about the kinds of publications you will be targeting. If you are writing for the consumer press – in other words, with a public readership – you will most certainly be supplying different information to that appropriate for trade magazines and industry newsletters. To take a basic example, if you were publicizing a new collection in a consumer magazine you would provide retail prices, while you would give wholesale prices to the trade press. You will often need to construct two slightly different press releases for the same story, possibly more.

Your press release should, naturally, be on your company letterhead, or if emailed, using your company email template. At the top, write 'Press Release' and the date.

Then write a headline. Don't try to be too clever, just informative. The headline should convey the story clearly and concisely. It must also grab the journalist's attention, otherwise they won't read any further. Spend some time on your headline.

The first paragraph is also crucial, as all essential information must be contained within it. So, if you are planning an exhibition, that means the venue details, dates and admission prices all need to appear here. Write the first paragraph as if it's the only thing that's going to be printed. In fact, it is a good idea to write each successive paragraph as if the following ones are going to be chopped off by the editor. This makes your story easy for even a lazy journalist to use, as they can print it as is, or just cut it down to the required length without changing a thing.

Each paragraph should provide more detail about the story that was essentially conveyed in the first paragraph. One of these should also contain a quote; journalists love to see a quote in a press release. I remember one editor referring to this as the obligatory 'Miss World' quote – in other words, something positive but not necessarily hugely meaningful. For example, 'Missy Smith says, "I'm very honoured to have won this prestigious award, especially as the competition was particularly fierce this year. I'm really looking forward to working with the organizers to make the touring exhibition a success!"' Of course, you might have something more interesting to say, and it will be even better if you can obtain a relevant quote from a third party to add credibility.

At the end of your story, write the word 'End' on a line of its own. Below that, if you want to provide some background information about your company, you may add a paragraph beginning 'Editor's Notes:' followed by details such as how long you have been in business, what your particular specialism is or anything else you feel is important.

Finally, add a 'For more information contact...' paragraph. Because many companies use outside agencies to handle their press releases, you need to be clear that you are the press contact. Provide your telephone number and email address here, even if they appear elsewhere in the document.

In your line of business, a professional-looking photograph is crucial. Bearing in mind that a cut-out product shot on a white background is preferable, include a photograph (.jpg is the most common format, as it is a universal and file sizes are relatively small). Don't clog up people's inboxes with huge files though. Photographs need to be 300 dpi at the size at which they will be printed; don't go overboard by providing an unsolicited poster-sized photo. If you are sending your release by post, include images along with the press release itself on a CD and print everything out as well.

Follow up your press release with another phone call, just to make sure it was received safely and to make yourself available should there be any questions.

ALERT EVERYONE ELSE WITH A NEWSLETTER

Emailed newsletters are a great way to stay connected with your audience and your wider network of colleagues, suppliers and friends. There are no set rules as to how often you should publish one, but bear in mind that you want to remind people you exist and are doing interesting things, without annoying them and causing them to unsubscribe. Two times a year seems to be about the norm for a small jewellery start-up, but once a month would not be unusual if you have a lot to say.

A newsletter can be as simple as a thoughtfully composed email consisting of perhaps three pieces of news (launch of a new collection, details of an upcoming exhibition, a customer survey...). With MailChimp or Constant Contact you can compose professional-looking newsletters either free of charge or for very reasonable rates. You may even wish to eschew the digital newsletter in favour of a printed one, but consider the printing and postage costs of this before taking the plunge.

Do things that make you an authority

In addition to doing interesting things, another way to build up your reputation is to present yourself as a figure of authority. Sure, you may have just started out in the jewellery business, but you know a lot more about it than most people. Presumably you're in this business because you have a keen interest in it and therefore have gathered a good deal of knowledge on the subject. Consider raising your game by getting involved in some of the following:

TEACHING: From lecturing at university level all the way through to evening classes at a local college, there are plenty of teaching opportunities out there. You might also consider starting up your own jewellery courses, taught from your own workshop.

PRESENTATIONS: Are you an expert in a particular technique? Do you have a unique take on jewellery that you could share with others? If public speaking doesn't fill you with dread then this is a great way to get your name around; keep your ear to the ground and take any speaking opportunities that come your way.

CONTRIBUTING TO A MAGAZINE OR NEWSLETTER: If you are good with words, you might enjoy writing a regular column for a trade or consumer publication. This not only gives you instant kudos, but ensures your name appears repeatedly in front of an audience and is therefore remembered.

Social media

Social media is yet another tool for reinforcing your brand and boosting your reputation. Like traditional media, it is a way to communicate your brand values, share interesting news and establish yourself as a figure of authority in your field. It also has the added advantage of allowing you to engage with your customers in a way not possible prior to the twenty-first century. This is good news for jewellery designers, many of whom trade as much on the strength of their personality as on the work they produce. Plus, as social media is increasingly geared towards the sharing of photos and videos, jewellers have a natural advantage in that creating beautiful things and images is their stock in trade.

As with traditional media, it is important to choose the social media platforms which are popular with your target audience.

For example, if your clients were all aged 40+, you wouldn't try to reach them through Teen Vogue. Likewise, each social media platform has a certain audience; you should make yourself aware of this information (easily done with a bit of online research) and plan your social media campaigns accordingly. These socio-demographic trends seem to come and go faster than you can say 'Myspace', so I will only provide the broadest of overviews here. Below is a rough guide to the types of social media platforms currently available, which might get you started thinking about how they can work for you.

BLOGGING: Publishing a blog is an easy and (usually) free way to increase publicity. It is basically the modern version of the traditional newsletter with the added bonus of enabling a two-way dialogue with your public and giving them the ability to share your messaging with their network. If you are lucky enough to be able to write in a clear, engaging and entertaining manner, it would be a shame not to take advantage of this profile-building opportunity. If writing is not your strong point, ask a trusted friend to proofread or edit your blog for you. There are several blogging platforms; currently on the market are wordpress.com, blog.com, blogger.com and many more. There is also Twitter, effectively a micro-blogger, which allows you to publish tiny bursts of up-to-the-second information with immense potential for expanding your online exposure.

SOCIAL AND BUSINESS NETWORKS: Facebook continues to dominate the social networking world. Generally, people have Facebook profiles and businesses have Facebook pages. However, some small businesses, especially those built around a single personality, use their personal pages to promote their businesses and encourage their clients to 'friend' them personally instead of setting up a separate business page. (Think carefully about how much you want your personal and business lives to merge before doing this!) The more usual route is to set up a personal profile and then add a page (not a profile) for your business. And as for pure business networking, LinkedIn is a useful platform for staying in touch with business contacts and raising your profile among your peers and associates. Note: This is not the place to post photos of what you got up to at the weekend (unless you were at a trade fair of course)!

PHOTO AND VIDEO SHARING: Video sharing sites such as YouTube and
Vimeo are used by businesses to build brands, generate
trust and drive traffic to their websites. For photo sharing,
Instagram is a hugely popular platform and can also be
used to share short video clips. Pinterest is a unique take
on photo sharing in that it allows you to collect images
online which you then curate into groups. (It is worth
noting that Pinterest's audience is predominantly female.)
A relative newcomer to the scene is Snapchat, which puts
a different angle on photo sharing in that images self-
destruct a few seconds after being viewed. Despite its
insalubrious beginnings, Snapchat is now embraced by
forward-thinking businesses as a credible and useful photo-
sharing tool, especially with its 'stories' function which
allows a 24-hour image lifespan. The marketing opportunities of this platform are currently in their infancy.

Take time to explore the above and do your own research online
to see which social media platforms are most relevant to your
business. Be sure to link up your various social media accounts
wherever possible so that each time you post to one platform it
shows up on the others. While you might want to dip your toe
in here and there and experiment with a few different platforms
to see what works for you, once you are comfortable you should
carefully coordinate your social media strategy for maximum reach
and impact. Just because it's free doesn't mean you shouldn't put
as much thought into social media as you would into traditional
printed materials. In fact, because the public is so overwhelmed
with social media messages, there is all the more reason to make
sure that yours really stand out.

7 Essential business skills

Every jewellery business is different, and you will develop your own way of operating your business over time. In fact, most of your business nous is likely to be learned on the job, not from books. However, there are certain fundamental skills best learned sooner rather than later, and the purpose of this chapter is to share some of these with you.

Essential time management

Although you might call yourself a jewellery designer/maker, you are actually much more than that. You are finance officer, marketing director, salesperson, cleaner and tea maker. Managing these very different tasks is a skill in itself, and there are many tools out there, digital and otherwise, which are designed to help you manage your time more effectively. My personal favourite is the Gantt chart.

Gantt charts are a great way of organizing your many roles and goals into one, easy-to-read sheet of paper. I use them all the time, whether planning the whole year, or just the weeks leading up to an important exhibition. Named after Henry Gantt, who popularized the concept in the 1910s, Gantt charts have taken many forms over the years and can be quite complex. I take a rather straightforward approach with mine as I find the beauty of the Gantt chart is in its simplicity. Feel free to experiment according to your needs.

Using Gantt charts to plan your year/month/week

My approach to time management can be summed up simply: at the end of every year, I plan the next year. At the end of every month, I plan the next month. At the end of every week, I plan the next week. If I am feeling particularly industrious, at the end of each day, I will plan the next day.

The genius of this convention is that it allows you to think big, but to then concentrate on the small. While your plan for the year might include the mammoth task of organizing a large exhibition, the related tasks on your monthly, and especially weekly, planners will be small and easy to accomplish.

Categorizing your tasks

The first step is to make a list of all the different categories that your various tasks fall into. Each of these will occupy one row of your chart. Your list might include, for example:

- Designing new work
- Making/production
- General administration
- Marketing/PR/advertising
- Research/inspiration
- Website updates
- Fairs
- Planning
- Research/training
- Other work (teaching, etc.)
- Holidays

Notice I have put 'Planning' in this list. This is essential – you must plan your planning! Other than that, feel free to alter the categories to suit you. If you find your home and work lives intertwine, you may want to include personal activities as well.

Year chart

Layout

I suggest starting out by laying out the entire year ahead, broken down into weeks. Your year chart will need fifty-two vertical columns, one for each week. If it doesn't make sense for your business to have a 52-week chart at this time, that's fine. The idea is to provide an overview of what you've got coming up. This has two uses. First, it provides an at-a-glance view of the year ahead. Second, it will provide the foundation for more detailed monthly and weekly planning.

If you are drawing up your chart in the middle of the year, it might make sense for you to just plan up until December and then start a new, year-long chart in January. Do whatever feels sensible. (The January–December calendar year is especially suited to jewellers as it ends with the December selling season.)

WORKSHEET: GANTT CHART - ONE YEAR

On this page is a blank year chart template for you to use. Because the number of full working weeks in any given month changes each year, I've left it to you to mark in the months.

PLANNING

It is rare that you will be entirely committed to one task or category for an entire week or month, but when you are, it means everything else gets put on hold. For me, the only events that have the power to demand 100 per cent of my time and attention are holidays. For this reason I always block these in solidly to illustrate that I'm completely booked up. It's a good idea to pencil in shows that you hope to get into, so you can hold those weeks free until further notice. How you choose to illustrate this is up to you.

Apart from fairs and holidays, your tasks will be more fluid and overlapping. You might plan, for example, to spend two months concentrating on designing a new collection. This doesn't mean that you stop everything else, but that you generally focus your time on that task while continuing all your other business

WORKSHEET: GANTT CHART - ONE YEAR

	JAN	FEB	MAR	APR	MAY	JUN	JUL	AUG	SEP	OCT	NOV	DEC
MAKING	orders	PRE ISLINGTON	FOR CHISWICK	FOR GROUP EXHIBITION	TOP-UPS	ONE-OFF FOR RCA		ORIGIN/GOLDSMITHS	SHOP → SHOP X	JULIE	(last minute orders....)	
NEW DESIGNS		EARRINGS			XMAS COLLECTION							
ADMIN (2 Thursdays/mo.)	‖‖‖	‖	‖	‖	‖	‖		‖	‖	‖	‖	‖
PRESS/P.R	*PR ISLINGTON		*PR OPEN STUDIO / BY EMAIL		OPEN STUDIO EMAIL	*PR ORIGIN G.S.		*PR OPEN STUDIO	ORIGIN/GS EMAIL			
WEBSITE						mark for Jul		UPDATE				
PLANNING (every Friday pm)	‖‖‖‖‖‖‖‖‖	‖‖	‖‖	‖‖	‖‖	‖‖		‖‖‖	‖‖‖	‖‖‖	‖‖‖	‖‖
FAIRS				ISLINGTON 17-20	6th AT BANK / 25-30 chiswick	OPEN STUDIO			ORIGIN	GOLDSMITH	OPEN STUDIO	
TEACHING (Tuesday eve.)	‖‖‖‖‖‖‖‖								‖‖‖‖‖‖‖‖			
TRAINING/ RESEARCH			‖‖‖‖‖ Rhino course					Residential course				
HOLIDAYS!							■	■				
EXHIBITION DATES +DEADLINES		BEST GS APPLICATION			7th GS PIECE FOR PHOTOGRAPHY			Collection 8th due to Leeds	SEPT: GALLERY X / 30th GALLERY	9th: SHOP X	JULIE ORDER DUE 11th / TOP-UPS due to Z	

activities as well. So, in the 'Designing new work' row, you might draw an arrow which extends throughout January and February with a note saying 'New aquamarine collection' or similar. (You will plan the collection in more detail when you move on to monthly and weekly charts.)

Carry on marking out your tasks and events in whatever way suits you. Use blocks of colour, arrows, stickers, whatever works. I've provided a blank chart should you wish to photocopy it, but you might want to create your own template, either digitally or by hand.

When you've filled in your chart for the year, the next step is to take it to the next level of detail.

Monthly chart

In your monthly chart, you basically take one month from your yearly chart and stretch it out to cover a whole page, allowing you to add more detail. Your monthly chart should contain the same

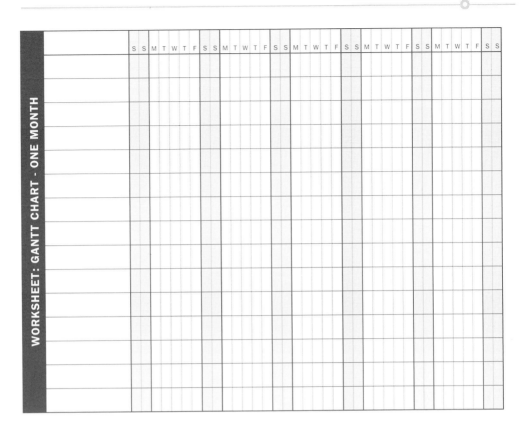

		S	S	M	T	W	T	F	S	S	M	T	W	T	F	S	S	M	T	W	T	F	S	S	M	T	W	T	F	S	S	M	T	W	T	F	S	S	M	T	W	T	F	S	S

WORKSHEET: GANTT CHART - ONE MONTH

rows as your year chart, so that you can easily transpose your activities.

At this level, your columns change from being weeks to actual days. So whereas January might have been roughly sketched out as a time for working on new designs, you can now designate which days you will dedicate (or at least mainly dedicate) to that task.

This is also a good place to block out time for those recurring administrative tasks such as paying bills and updating your website. As a rule I like to set aside one day a week where I do nothing but admin, and one day a month to update my website. Don't forget to schedule in some research and training days, whether once a month or once a week. It's an important part of staying creative.

In your monthly planner, don't forget to schedule in time to plan the following month. I normally put a little 'x' on the last working day of the month with a note to plan the next month.

A template is provided above.

WORKSHEET: GANTT CHART - ONE MONTH

FEBRUARY	31	1	2	3	4	5	6	7	8	9	10	11	12	13	14	15	16	17	18	19	20	21	22	23	24	25	26	27	28							
	S	S	M	T	W	T	F	S	S	M	T	W	T	F	S	S	M	T	W	T	F	S	S	M	T	W	T	F	S	S	M	T	W	T	F	S	S
MAKING		new design		☒					☒		☒					☒	☒		☒					☒	☒												
NEW DESIGNS		☒	☒		amryp		☒																														
ADMIN (2 THURSDAYS/Mo.)		..												☒														☒									
PRESS/PR																																					
WEBSITE																																					
PLANNING (every Friday pm)							☒							☒							☒							☒									
FAIRS																																					
TEACHING (Tues. eve.)			☒							☒							☒							☒													
TRAINING/ RESEARCH																	☒								☒												
HOLIDAYS																																					
EXHIBITION DATES/DEADLINES															☒ = Filling GS Application.					• POST GS APPLICATION																		

Weekly chart

Once you zoom in to the next level, planning your week, you will probably be writing your tasks down in your diary rather than in a chart. I'm not going to tell you how to do this, as you probably have your own system. The important thing is that, when planning your week, you refer to your monthly planner to see what you should be working on each day. Take this information and then break it down into smaller chunks and daily to-do lists. Each time you tick something off the list, you'll know you've made one small step towards the completion of a much bigger task which you set out initially when planning your year.

Put a note on every single Friday in your diary to plan the following week.

Essential money management

Whenever I am asked what my one piece of advice would be to jewellery start-ups, my answer is the same: do a cash flow forecast. It sounds boring, but it is extremely important. If you fail to complete this relatively simple task, you have no idea if your business even has a chance of staying afloat. (This section is titled 'Essential money management' because it really is essential!)

Cash flow forecast

A cash flow forecast is like a bank statement, except that it shows the future of your bank account, not the past. Just like a bank statement, it shows money going in and out of your account each month. Unlike a bank statement, however, it is based on guesswork rather than fact. In this respect the process can seem overwhelming, but don't worry – it's perfectly normal to feel a sense of trepidation.

The whole point of forecasting your cash flow is to see how much money you are likely to have in your bank account in the months ahead. Why is this important? Because you don't want to run out of it; if that happens, you can't carry on running your business. With no cash, you're stuck; you can't buy materials, pay your workshop rent or pay yourself.

The problem is, you need to spend money to make money; in order to make any sales, you're going to have to be prepared to invest some cash up front. The question is, will your business survive until your investment starts to pay off?

A cash flow can tell you:

- whether you can afford to make the stock for an exhibition;
- how much S.O.R. you can take on;
- whether it would make financial sense to take on an assistant;
- whether you can afford a bigger studio space;
- whether you can afford to quit your part-time job.

If the forecast is all doom and gloom, it's time to rethink your business strategy. If it looks promising, then you know you've got a good chance of succeeding if everything goes according to plan.

How to do a cash flow forecast

SET UP YOUR SPREADSHEET

If you're not yet familiar with Microsoft Excel, or similar

spreadsheet applications, now is the time to learn. With free alternatives such as Open Office (www.openoffice.org), there is no excuse for using pen and paper for this exercise. You'll soon see why.

Refer to the example spreadsheet on page 119 and set up your template in a similar manner. The next 12 months should run across the top. (You can create your forecast for as few or as many months as you wish, but a year is typical.) Down the left-hand side, list your categories of income and expenditure. It is important to include a total income and total expenditure row as well.

On the example spreadsheet, all the numbers shown in bold are the results of formulas. All the non-bold numbers were entered manually. Each cell in the total income row, for example, shows the sum of the two income cells above it. Likewise, the total expenditure cells show the sum totals of the cells above. This way, any changes you make to any of your income or expenditure figures will automatically be reflected in the totals.

At the bottom are three very important rows: opening balance, monthly cash flow and closing balance. The only number you will manually enter into these rows is the opening balance of the very first month. If you are starting from scratch with a new bank account, this number will be zero. All other cells in these rows contain formulas as follows:

- With the exception of the very first month, the opening balance is always the same as the previous month's closing balance. So set February's opening balance as the sum of January's closing balance, and so on.
- The monthly cash flow is the sum of the month's total income minus total expenditure. If your monthly income is greater than your expenditure, the result will be a positive number. If, on the other hand, you've spent more than you've earned, it will be negative.
- The closing balance is simply the sum of the previous two cells, the opening balance and monthly cash flow. If your cash flow is a positive number, your closing balance will be greater than your opening balance. If your cash flow is negative, your bank balance will decrease and you will have a lower figure.

Once you've set up your template, complete with cell formulas, it's time to start entering some figures.

INCOME

The first thing to do is to estimate how much money you'll have coming into your account each month as the result of sales. This goes in the first row. In order to estimate this with any degree of accuracy you'll have to think carefully about the year ahead. How, where and when do you expect to sell your work? What fairs are you planning on doing? Do you have any commissions lined up? Remember, if you are doing any S.O.R., you may not see the cash from your Christmas sales until as late as February or even March. This is because galleries often extend their return policies during Christmas, therefore delaying payment to you. A cash flow forecast is all about when that money hits your bank account, which is not necessarily when the sale is made.

The other income row is for any money that is not the result of sales. This could be capital investment (money you've saved up to start your business, as shown by the figure in the example), income from teaching, perhaps a loan or a grant – any money that will appear in your business bank account but that is not the result of sales.

EXPENDITURE

You'll notice that the categories of expenditure are pretty much the same as those used in the annual overheads worksheet on page 29. But there are some extra lines here. That's because your cash flow forecast is about all of the cash moving in and out of your account, not just your overheads.

The most notable extra category here is materials. (Materials are not considered overheads because they are a variable, billable expense, whereas overheads tend to be the fixed costs of keeping your business running.) For the purpose of a cash flow forecast, however, none of this matters. All that concerns us here is how much money is coming into the account, and how much is going out – and when. For jewellers working with precious metals, materials are a common source of cash flow troubles, especially when faced with having to make lots of stock for a retail fair or an S.O.R.

Tax is another important category. Find out from your government website or your accountant when your tax bill is likely to fall due and roughly how much you might expect to pay.

If you're just setting up in business, you will inevitably incur extra start-up costs for things such as new tools and equipment, telephone installation, packaging and marketing materials, so remember to include these figures in your estimates.

How to use your cash flow forecast
KEEP YOUR EYE ON THE BOTTOM LINE

If you've set up all your cell functions correctly you'll notice that the last three lines constantly adjust to reflect the results of your income and expenditure. Pay special attention to your closing balance – the bottom line. (The idea is to keep this above zero!)

TROUBLESHOOTING

How is the bottom line looking? If it's a positive number at all times, that's great. But what do you do if you see it going into the red? Start by trying to identify the root of the problem. Some common causes are:

- taking on too much S.O.R.;
- taking on too many exhibitions in a short space of time;
- disappointing sales;
- sales concentrated around one season;
- underpricing;
- failing to set aside money for tax.

One way of addressing the problem is to arrange an overdraft with your bank. It's a good idea to have a pre-arranged overdraft anyway, just to have a cushion against unforeseen difficulties. Talk to your bank manager to see what they are prepared to offer you. You might find that a short-term loan is a better solution, for example if you see yourself going heavily overdrawn for just a short space of time.

An even better idea is to see if you can come up with a positive course of action to prevent your bank balance from dipping in the first place. For example, say you are spending thousands of pounds on materials in order to stock a dozen or so shops on an S.O.R. basis, and this is causing a cash flow problem. You could solve this in a number of ways.

First, you could try to get some of the shops to buy. You might even be able to come to an agreement whereby a shop agrees to purchase half of the stock and take the rest on consignment. It's not unusual for a shop to buy smaller pieces that are sure sellers, and then ask for a couple of big showpieces on S.O.R.

If this isn't an option, you might just need to grow your business more slowly, adding one new stockist every few months and waiting for the first one to start paying off before adding the second. To see if this will work, adjust your numbers to reflect this

CASH FLOW FORECAST	Jan	Feb	Mar	Apr	May	Jun	Jul	Aug	Sep	Oct	Nov	Dec
INCOME												
Sales	4,000	2,000	1,000	1,000	1,000	1,000	1,500	1,500	2,000	4,000	4,000	3,000
Other	300	300	300	300	300				300	300	300	300
Total income	4,300	2,300	1,300	1,300	1,300	1,000	1,500	1,500	2,300	4,300	4,300	3,300
EXPENDITURE												
Rent	300	300	300	300	300	300	300	300	300	300	300	300
Heat, power	40	40	40	40	40	40	40	40	40	40	40	40
Telephone and internet	30	30	30	30	30	30	30	30	30	30	30	30
Insurance			350									
Motor expenses								50				
Printed stationery				200					200			
General office supplies	25	25	25	25	25	25	25	25	25	25	25	25
Photography				300					300			
Marketing, advertising								100	100			
Website	30	30	30	30	30	30	30	30	30	30	30	30
Exhibitions			250	300			900		750		100	
Packaging								250				
Postage, shipping	10	10	20	20	20	20	20	20	20	50	50	50
Travel and subsistence	20	20	20	20	20	20	20	20	20	20	20	20
Loose tools	20	20	20	20	20	20	20	20	40	40	20	20
Bank charges	10	10	10	10	10	10	10	10	10	10	10	10
Professional fees									400			
Drawings	1,000	1,000	1,000	1,000	1,000	1,000	1,000	1,000	1,000	1,000	1,000	1,000
Materials	300	300	300	300	300	300	300	300	600	600	300	300
Tax, National Insurance	10	8	10	8	10	8	10	8	10	8	3,000	8
Other												
Total expenditure	1,795	1,793	2,405	2,603	1,805	1,803	2,705	2,203	3,875	2,153	4,925	1,833
Opening balance	2,000	4,505	5,012	3,907	2,604	2,099	1,296	91	-612	-2,187	-40	-665
Monthly cash flow	2,505	507	-1,105	-1,303	-505	-803	-1,205	-703	-1,575	2,147	-625	1,467
Closing balance	4,505	5,012	3,907	2,604	2,099	1,296	91	-612	-2,187	-40	-665	802

new, imagined scenario and see if things look better or worse. Your material costs will be lower but your sales will be too.

A cash flow forecast can be the bringer of bad news. You may find out that you can't afford that new workshop, or to do that exhibition, or to pay yourself as much as you'd like. But the process of doing the forecast enables you to solve these problems before they become a reality. Congratulate yourself for undertaking this exercise, which so many new business owners fail to do.

On the other hand, a cash flow forecast can show you, in financial terms, the potential growth and profitability that can come with a relatively modest initial investment, for example an ambitious marketing campaign, or a new, luxury collection. With this knowledge you can forge ahead confidently, numbers firmly in hand.

MAINTENANCE

It's a good idea, especially in the critical early stages of a business, not only to do an initial cash flow forecast, but to then update it on a monthly basis to make sure you're keeping on track.

Once you've completed your forecast, make a copy of the file and call it something like 'Cash flow actual'. Keep all your predicted figures intact for now.

When you receive your bank statement for the first month (let's say it's January), replace your estimated January numbers with real ones taken from your bank statement. You'll have to go through your statement and identify exactly what each outgoing figure is for, so that you can determine how much was spent in each category. When you've finished, January's closing balance on your cash flow forecast should match the 31 January balance on your bank statement. If there is a discrepancy, go back to see what you've missed.

Has January gone to plan? Were there any expenses you hadn't planned for? Did you have any sales or other income you hadn't expected? Is January's closing balance higher or lower than predicted? Look at the months ahead and notice how the last three lines of your forecast are affected as a result of January's activities.

Repeat the process at the end of February. Continue plugging in real figures at the end of each month, and keep an eye on how this affects your future.

If things aren't going to plan, do something about it. And whatever solution you come up with, whether it be taking out a loan or just putting more effort into your sales, amend your predicted figures accordingly.

A cash flow forecast should be a source of comfort, not anxiety. Rather than burying your head in the sand and hoping for the best, put your mind at ease by keeping a watchful eye on your cash flow month by month. Forewarned is forearmed!

Basic bookkeeping

It is a statutory requirement that you keep records of your business transactions. If you are a sole trader, this needn't be complicated. At its most basic, your system need only contain two things: a sales ledger and a purchase ledger. Bear in mind, however, that if you decide to trade as a company, the rules are stricter and you will need to enlist the help of an accountant to prepare your records for you.

SALES LEDGER

This is a record of all your sales, which you can list manually or with a spreadsheet programme. The columns you need are:

- Date of invoice
- Invoice number
- Customer name
- Amount
- Tax
- Total
- Date paid
- Payment method
- Remarks

Your accountant will need this list at the end of the tax year, and you will need to refer to it regularly, especially the date paid column, to make sure your clients have paid you on time.

PURCHASE LEDGER

Likewise, you will need to keep track of all your expenses with a list. The purchase ledger should have the following columns:

- Date of invoice (if relevant)
- Invoice number (if relevant)
- Supplier name
- Amount
- Tax
- Total
- Date paid
- Payment method
- Remarks

You should also analyse your expenses in several columns, each denoting a different category of expenditure. If your business is very small, you may not be required to provide such detailed information in your tax return.

However, it's a good idea to be able to see where your money is being spent, and it will be useful in terms of your cash flow reports.

Update your purchase ledger regularly! It's easy if you set aside time weekly or monthly to do it. Don't make the mistake of waiting until the end of the tax year and entering an entire year's worth of receipts all at once!

8 Planning for growth and sustainability

This chapter is intended for those who already have a reasonably established business. If you're just starting out, you may want to give this chapter only the most cursory reading lest you become overwhelmed with the question of 'Where do I go next?' before you've even decided where to start!

There will probably come a stage in your career where you hit a plateau. You may have been successfully growing your client base for years, only to find that the expansion has ceased. Or perhaps your work is stocked so widely that you can't think of a single new retailer to approach. Or, like many craft practitioners, you may have found yourself in a position where you are working every waking hour just to keep your business afloat, but still struggling to make ends meet.

These are just a few ways in which a business can find itself stuck. While it is good to know how to get out of these situations, it is obviously better to avoid them altogether. For this reason you should set aside time to plan for the growth (if you do indeed want to expand) and sustainability of your business. By sustainability I mean creating a business that can sustain itself (as opposed to sustaining the environment, which is a different matter altogether) – in other words, a business that can survive and prosper in the long term.

Growth and sustainability through diversity

Diversity is a crucial concept. Understanding the importance of this fundamental principle just may be the best thing you can do for the long-term sustainability of your business.

What is diversity? In this context it means having a variety of products and/or services on offer, or selling to a variety of markets. The act of diversification refers to adding new products/services to your range (product development), or broadening your sales reach to new market segments or territories (market development).

It is well known that increasing diversity reduces the risk of financial loss. Why? Simply put, it's not a good idea to have all of your eggs in one basket. This is true whether you are a global brand name or a part-time jeweller working from your kitchen table. So, if you really want to create a more sustainable business for the long term, you should think about diversification. Likewise, if you want your business to grow and expand, diversification can open doors to help you achieve this. For these reasons, I would argue that the best way to move your business forward in a way that increases its chances of survival as well as its success is to a) identify the areas in which your business is undiversified, and b) introduce diversity to these areas.

Risks of an undiversified product offering (i.e. a narrow range of work)

Small jewellery businesses, by their very nature, tend to be undiversified in many ways and, although many achieve geographical diversity by establishing sales relationships abroad, most makers offer a relatively narrow product offering. This is necessary in order to establish oneself as a designer/maker; as discussed elsewhere in this book, achieving a reputation for a unique and distinctive style is how you get noticed and differentiate yourself from the market. The flip side to this narrow focus is that, by investing your time and efforts in a very specific type of work, you are taking on certain risks such as:

- your style of work falling out of favour;
- a sharp increase or decrease in the value of your chosen materials;
- ethical issues arising relating to the sourcing of your materials;
- your unique production methods being made redundant by new technology, thereby detracting from the value of your work;
- your unique materials becoming widely available, thereby detracting from the uniqueness and value of your work;
- somebody copying your style, or innocently producing work in a similar style, which draws customers away from you;
- a decrease in demand for work in your price range.

The solution: product development – Most jewellers are engaged in some level of product development already because they are constantly adding new designs to their existing range. However, to really bring diversity to your offering means to go further than that and produce work which is different in terms of style, materials or price points. It could also mean introducing a new service for your customers which complements your existing business. One must take extreme care, however, when introducing new work; if not thought through carefully, this could have a negative effect on your brand (see Chapter 6). Whatever new products you introduce, they must stay true to your brand values. Alternatively, you could consider bringing out a new line of work under a completely different brand name so as not to confuse your existing message.

For the ultimate diversification, don't rule out developing a product which isn't jewellery at all, especially if you find your unique tools and set-up lend themselves to such an idea. (This way you even have some level of protection should the entire jewellery industry collapse!)

If you start making work that is either very different in style or price in comparison to your present work, you are likely to be selling it to a different breed of customer. In other words, you will be undertaking market development (more on this below) as well as product development. You may also win additional business from your existing customers who have already reached saturation point with your current work.

Risks of an undiversified market (i.e. risks of a narrow client or stockist base, especially if they are all in the same area)

Most jewellers naturally start selling their work through a few shops in the area where they live, which is the logical thing to do. However, if you remain focused on very few retailers, especially if they are concentrated in one geographical area, you will face certain risks associated with having an undiversified market, both in terms of the type of customer you are targeting as well as their geographical spread. Risks associated with a narrow market include:

- one of your retailers (representing a large percentage of your sales) going bust;
- a change in local tastes negatively impacting your sales;
- a decline in the local economy affecting your sales;
- decreased sales from one of your retailers due to a change in management, changes to pedestrian traffic, or other unknowns.

The solution: Market development – These risks can be reduced through market development, that is, targeting retail and wholesale customers in new markets. If you have only a few retailers, this could simply mean approaching new stockists. Better yet, if you only sell locally, you will achieve greater diversification by expanding into other geographical areas. For the highest market diversification possible, you might want to consider selling in other countries where tastes, economies and other local factors will differ hugely from those of your existing market (in other words, markets which are *uncorrelated* to your existing ones).

The advantages to market development are obvious – more customers means more sales. Another plus is that, unlike product development, market development does not threaten to confuse your brand message; whereas bringing out entirely new and different product lines can dilute or even damage your brand, expanding into new markets does not cause any such conflict. Perhaps it is for this reason that so many designers/makers choose to grow their businesses by expanding into new territories while sticking to their existing product offering.

There are potential disadvantages to market development, however. It takes a lot more time and effort to find a new customer in a new market (especially abroad) than to sell to existing clients. Plus, without prior knowledge of a particular market, you won't have an understanding of that market's tastes, preferences, tolerances and quirks; this only comes with experience.

Exploiting strengths and opportunities

We have now seen how product and market development can help to grow your business while simultaneously making it more sustainable. But how do you decide which route to pursue – product development, market development or both? And in what way? The opportunities are endless!

Identify your strengths

One answer is to simply play to your strengths. This may sound obvious, but it is easy to forget that we each have certain areas in which we have an advantage over the competition. (Most jewellers can give you a list as long as their arm of all the obstacles they face, but aren't quite so quick to recognize their own strengths!) It is worthwhile taking some time to identify these – as a person and as a business – and not just the obvious ones to do with your technical skill and design sense. The following categories might help trigger some ideas:

Tangible resources (materials, workshop, storage space, property, tools, other assets...)

Intangible resources (reputation, branding, specialist knowledge, access to rare materials or specialist equipment, intellectual property, time...)

Financial resources (cash, credit line...)

Practical skills (general and specialist jewellery skills, unique techniques that you have developed yourself, design skills, skills gained through hobbies/interests...)

Other skills (business, languages, people skills, IT, photography, social media, skills gained through a previous career...)

Relationships/connections (friends, family, clients, suppliers, networking groups, other jewellers/craftspeople, established presence at certain fairs/exhibitions, relations abroad...)

Once you have identified your strengths (and feel free to include those with no apparent relation to jewellery), the next step is to think about which of these are particularly rare or unique to you. The most obvious would be your distinctive jewellery style. What other rare skills, assets and relationships do you have? Could any of these be used towards product development or market development, or both? As a further brainstorming exercise, try taking two of your strengths (the more unique, the better) and think about what is achievable by combining these. You might be surprised at what you find!

Identify the opportunities

Another way of approaching the same question is to look outwards rather than inwards, and try to identify opportunities in the market which you can take advantage of. Ask yourself the following questions:

Gaps in the market – Is there a product or service which customers want but which nobody seems to be offering? Is there a particular type of customer whose needs are not addressed by the jewellery currently on offer?

Social trends – Are there changes in society which might give rise to the need for a certain product or service which does not yet exist?

Technology – Are there advances in technology which make new products or services possible?

Legal – Have changes in law or regulation (perhaps to do with the materials you use) changed?

Economic factors – Can you turn recent changes in the economy (for example, an increase or decrease in the price of precious metals) to your advantage?

Adaptability – Are your tools and/or working methods suited to making something besides jewellery?

Grants and awards – Is there a grant or award programme which may be able to give you a boost?

New ways of targeting customers – Is there a way of reaching customers that you haven't tried, or are you able to invent a new way of doing this?

Collaborations – Do you have a friend or colleague who you could join forces with to create a new product or service, or to put together a cross-referral programme, enabling each of you to target the other's customers?

Complementary products and services – Is there a service you could offer your customers which they would appreciate – perhaps something that makes use of your other skills? (Remember the days before bookshops had coffee shops in them? This is a classic example!)

Matching up strengths and opportunities

Having looked inwards at your strengths, and outwards at opportunities in the market, see if you can match any of these up and identify which opportunities you, bearing in mind your unique set of skills and resources, would be best placed to take advantage of. In other words, if you have an established business making bold, contemporary necklaces in brightly-coloured plastics and you spot a gap in the market for traditional gem-set rings in platinum, you are unlikely to be the person most suited to fill that gap (unless of course you have a history of traditional goldsmithing from a previous life – in which case your biggest challenge would be the branding issue as discussed in Chapter 6). If, on the other hand, you can spot an opportunity which you are already partially geared up for, it's going to be easier for you to exploit that opportunity than a competitor who doesn't have the necessary knowledge or skills.

Cash flow forecasting for growth

While diversifying your business is a good way to approach growth and sustainability, be warned that too much growth or change, too quickly, can actually be dangerous, particularly in terms of cash flow. It is not uncommon, for example, for young businesses to find themselves strapped for cash, having invested it all in inventory and other assets or expenses which are needed to expand. This is called 'overtrading'. For jewellers, especially those working in precious materials, this usually manifests itself in the problem of having to produce the work before you are paid for it. In some cases, you might have to wait a very long time to recoup these expenses, especially if you work on a S.O.R. basis or if you sell to large retailers which can have long payment times. For these reasons it is crucial you map out how your intended growth/ sustainability strategy will affect your bank balance by crafting your plan very carefully and reflecting this in a cash flow forecast. If the figures reveal that your plan requires a sizeable injection of cash at a certain point, you'll know how much finance is required, and when. And if your forecast reveals that your plan is actually going to lose more money than it makes, then the exercise will have saved you a lot of hardship.

If you don't know how to do a cash flow forecast, please go back to Chapter 7 where this is explained in detail.

Setting up your spreadsheet

When planning a special project or change in direction, it is a good idea to draw up a separate cash flow worksheet which isolates this activity. (I will call this your 'project cash flow'.) Create your project cash flow as a separate tab in your Excel workbook. Then, to see the effect of the project on your overall cash flow, insert a line into your business-as-usual (BAU) worksheet which takes the monthly net cash flow line from your project cash flow, as per the illustration below.

BUSINESS-AS-USUAL CASH FLOW (PLUS IMPACT OF PROJECT CASH FLOW)

	Jan	Feb	Mar	Apr	May	Jun	Jul	Aug	Sep	Oct	Nov	Dec
INCOME												
Sales	4,000	2,000	1,000	1,000	1,000	1,000	1,500	1,500	2,000	4,000	4,000	3,000
Other	300	300	300	300	300				300	300	300	300
Total BAU income	4,300	2,300	1,300	1,300	1,300	1,000	1,500	1,500	2,300	4,300	4,300	3,300
EXPENDITURE												
Rent	300	300	300	300	300	300	300	300	300	300	300	300
Heat, power	40	40	40	40	40	40	40	40	40	40	40	40
Telephone and internet	30	30	30	30	30	30	30	30	30	30	30	30
Insurance			350									
Motor expenses								50				
Printed stationery				200					200			
General office supplies	25	25	25	25	25	25	25	25	25	25	25	25
Photography				300					300			
Marketing, advertising								100	100			
Website	30	30	30	30	30	30	30	30	30	30	30	30
Exhibitions			250	300				900	750	100		
Packaging									250			
Postage, shipping	10	10	20	20	20	20	20	20	20	50	50	50
Travel and subsistence	20	20	20	20	20	20	20	20	20	20	20	20
Loose tools	20	20	20	20	20	20	20	20	40	40	20	20
Bank charges	10	10	10	10	10	10	10	10	10	10	10	10
Professional fees									400			
Drawings	1,000	1,000	1,000	1,000	1,000	1,000	1,000	1,000	1,000	1,000	1,000	1,000
Materials	300	300	300	300	300	300	300	300	600	600	300	300
Tax, National Insurance	10	8	10	8	10	8	10	8	10	8	3,000	8
Other												
Total BAU expenditure	1,795	1,793	2,405	2,603	1,805	1,803	2,705	2,203	3,875	2,153	4,925	1,833
Opening balance	2,000	4,505	5,012	3,907	2,354	1,849	46	-2,679	-4,702	-9,057	-2,240	-1,075
Monthly BAU cash flow	2,505	507	-1,105	-1,303	-505	-803	-1,205	-703	-1,575	2,147	-625	1,467
Monthly project cash flow	0	0	0	-250	0	-1,000	-1,520	-1,320	-2,780	4,670	1,790	1,890
Closing balance	4,505	5,012	3,907	2,354	1,849	46	-2,679	-4,702	-9,057	-2,240	-1,075	2,282

PROJECT CASH FLOW

	Jan	Feb	Mar	Apr	May	Jun	Jul	Aug	Sep	Oct	Nov	Dec
INCOME												
Sales										6,000	2,000	2,000
Other												
Total project income	0	0	0	0	0	0	0	0	0	6,000	2,000	2,000
EXPENDITURE												
Rent												
Heat, power												
Telephone and internet												
Insurance												
Motor expenses												
Printed stationery												
General office supplies									10	10	10	10
Photography								300				
Marketing, advertising												
Website									750			
Exhibitions				250					1,000		100	
Packaging						500						
Postage, shipping											100	100
Travel and subsistence										300		
Loose tools							20	20	20	20		
Bank charges												
Professional fees												
Drawings												
Materials						500	500	500	500	500		
Tax, National Insurance												
Other						500	500	500	500	500		
Total project expenditure	0	0	0	250	0	1,000	1,520	1,320	2,780	1,330	210	110
Opening balance	0	0	0	0	-250	-250	-1,250	-2,770	-4,090	-6,870	-2,200	-410
Monthly project cash flow	0	0	0	-250	0	-1,000	-1,520	-1,320	-2,780	4,670	1,790	1,890
Closing balance	0	0	0	-250	-250	-1,250	-2,770	-4,090	-6,870	-2,200	-410	1,480

Normally if planning a big change you'd want to draw up a business plan and corresponding cash flow forecast for the next three years or so. (If you don't know how to write a business plan, there are plenty of online resources to help you do this. A good place to start is www.startupdonut.co.uk, as are the 'Business and self-employed' pages of www.gov.uk.)

For the sake of illustration, the example on page 130 shows a relatively small project which only has a one-year duration. Imagine you have a fairly established business designing and making silver jewellery. You decide to diversify your product offering by bringing out an 18-carat gold range which you intend to launch at an exhibition taking place in October. After some careful planning you estimate that, if the work is well received, you will take around £6,000 in sales at the exhibition itself, with another £4,000 worth of orders coming through in the run-up to Christmas.

The exhibition organizers require a deposit in April and the final payment in September. You don't live near the venue so will have to pay for travel and accommodation. You will need to spend the summer/autumn designing and making the new collection which will be costly in terms of materials. Because you are already quite busy, you will also need to farm out some of the fabrication work. (This expense is included in 'other'.) To promote the range, you plan to have a page dedicated to it on your website, so some development will be required. Your existing packaging is very basic and not really suitable for a luxury range, so new boxes and bags will have to be ordered.

Ideally, you should do three different forecasts reflecting the best- and worst-case scenarios and a middling one showing how you expect things to go. So, in addition to the one shown in the example, you should do one forecast which assumes you sell nothing at the exhibition, and one that assumes the show is more successful than expected.

Analysing the results

PROJECT CASH FLOW

Looking at your project cash flow, you can see that it puts a real strain on resources throughout the year, with several months of negative flows right through to September. Fortunately, this is compensated for by sales income in October, November and December. What is very important to note is that the 'closing balance' figure in December is positive at £1,480. This means that, if all goes to plan, your project will break even in December and will ultimately add £1,480 to your bank balance. If you are happy with that, then the project is worth doing.

However, £1,480 does not leave you much room for error. If your sales are £1,480 less than expected, or your expenses are £1,480 more, your project will not make a profit. This is why it is important to try out best- and worst-case scenarios. On the other hand, your inflows probably wouldn't stop at the end of December. The exhibition would likely have positive knock-on effects long after the year in question. Clients may look you up years later, having picked up a card at the show. You are also likely to come away with unsold stock which can be sold at a later date. These things are impossible to predict however, so don't worry about them for now – just make sure your short to medium term cash flow forecast is in order.

Business-as-usual cash flow

The real proof of whether your project is viable can be seen when you consider its impact on your overall business-as-usual (BAU) cash flow. Those months of negative flows really start to take their toll in the run-up to the show, with your bank balance going over £9,000 into the red in September. This is not necessarily a problem if you have access to finance. However, if you aren't able to get a loan or other funds to cover this, or if you just don't feel comfortable about that level of debt, you may want to rethink your plans. The important thing is that you have taken the time to forecast the situation and can therefore take steps to address it (as discussed in Chapter 7).

Another issue highlighted by this autumnal dip is the fact that your new project operates on a similar seasonal cycle to your existing activities – in other words, it involves building up inventory over the summer and autumn months, followed by strong sales at the end of the year. You could consider smoothing out your cash flow by instead launching your range at an exhibition taking place in spring/summer rather than autumn/winter.

Finally, it is worth pointing out that, although the project hasn't had any effect on your tax payment in the year in question, it will affect the amount of tax you have to pay next year.

Worst-case scenario

Please do not neglect to do your worst-case scenario forecast. It's very simple: just replace all those nice sales figures with zeros! Now ask yourself, would my business be able to survive this? If the answer is no, then proceed only if you are comfortable with the idea of risking your entire business for the sake of £1,480!

A final note about planning

Planning is a skill just like any other, and should become part of your routine. As you build your business, you will develop and hone this skill, adapting and changing your methods as you go. As you gain experience, forecasting will become easier and planning will become integral to your day-to-day activities. Take your business forward with open eyes. Make sure you understand what you are doing and why, and what you expect the outcome to be. If it works on paper, it just might work in real life!

Resources

Sample documents

Sale-or-return agreement

Many shops will have their own S.O.R. agreements which they will require you to sign, but surprisingly many will not. Follow the one provided here, or draw up your own, but never provide work on S.O.R. without some sort of agreement on paper. It's best to get this agreed before you send the delivery. Send two copies and have the stockist send one back to you, signed, for your records.

Sale-or-return delivery note

Always provide a comprehensive delivery note when providing work on S.O.R. (or on any basis, for that matter). Send two copies with the delivery, and request that one is signed and sent back to you so that you have proof of delivery. The document should contain the following columns:

CODE: Each piece you supply should have a code. There is no set way to code your pieces, so devise a system that works for you. This could be as simple as starting with 0001 and numbering them consecutively. Or you might employ a system whereby the type of piece, materials and collection are reflected in the code. For example, SF-N-01-S might stand for Sunflower (SF) Necklace (N) number 1 (01), in silver (S).

DESCRIPTION: This can be either the name of a piece or a description of its physical characteristics.

MATERIALS: It is important to be clear about what the piece is made of. It is your legal responsibility to describe materials accurately, especially in the case of precious metals and stones. With diamonds you would also be expected to state the carat weight, cut, colour and clarity.

SAMPLE SALE-OR-RETURN AGREEMENT

Sale-Or-Return Agreement

Supplier: Smith & Bloggs, Unit 1, The Studios, 123 High Street, Anywheresville, AY1 2SV

Stockist: The Jewellery Shop, 456 High Street, Anytown, AT8 5JS

Responsibilities of the Supplier

The Supplier shall:

- Supply goods of saleable quality along with wholesale prices
- In respect of any item sold by the Stockist, repair and, if reasonable, replace all faulty items
- Respond to requests for quotes efficiently and accurately
- Keep the Stockist informed of any change in contact details and any periods of unavailability
- Be responsible for the safe delivery of goods to the Stockist

Responsibilities of the Stockist

The Stockist shall:

- Keep the work in good, clean condition
- Keep work on display at all times (either the entire collection or a good representation of it)
- Compensate the Supplier for any loss of, or damage to, work
- Inform the Supplier in good time when goods have been sold
- Pay the Supplier no later than the end of the month after which the goods have been sold
- Be responsible for the safe return of unsold goods to the Supplier
- Comply with reasonable requests from the Supplier if stock is needed to be temporarily 'borrowed back' for photography or other purposes

The Work

- The goods will remain the property of the Supplier until sold by the Stockist who shall not be entitled to alter the items in any way
- The Supplier retains copyright of all work

Signed

On behalf of Smith & Bloggs
Jane Smith

On behalf of The Jewellery Shop

_____
Printed name

_____   _____
Signature   Date   Signature   Date

UNIT PRICE: This is your wholesale price, exclusive of any tax.

QUANTITY: If you only work in one-offs, you won't need this column.

SUBTOTAL: This is the unit price multiplied by the quantity.

You may also want to include an 'Image' column with a photograph of each piece to make referencing easier.

SAMPLE SALE-OR-RETURN DELIVERY NOTE

Smith & Bloggs
Unit 1, The Studios
123 High Street
Anywheresville
AY1 2SV
Tel: 012 345 6789
jane@smithandbloggs.biz
www.smithandbloggs.biz

To:
The Jewellery Shop
456 High Street
Anytown
AT8 5JS

Date

Code	Description	Unit Price	Quantity	Subtotal
0782	One-off necklace, small oval shapes with leaf pattern	£426	1	£426
0522	One-off necklace, leaf shapes with squares, 50" long	£1,228	1	£1,228
0612	One-off 'Scribble' bracelet	£320	1	£320
0613	One-off 'Scribble' bracelet	£208	1	£208
SFNL01-S	'Sunflower' necklace	£76	2	£152
SFBL01-S	'Sunflower' bracelet	£49	2	£98
SFER01-S	'Sunflower' earrings	£24	2	£48
Total			**10**	**£2,480**

All work is provided on a sale-or-return basis and remains the property of Smith & Bloggs until paid for in full. Full compensation for any loss or damage to these items shall be paid by The Jewellery Shop to Smith & Bloggs. Please note all prices are subject to Value Added Tax at the prevailing rate.

Received in good condition by:

Printed name	Signature	Date

Invoice

Invoices are important, not only for your own records but for tax purposes, so make sure they are accurate. An invoice must contain:

YOUR TRADING NAME ADDRESS: This is your trading address.

INVOICE NUMBER: It is best practice to use a sequential numbering system.

INVOICE DATE: This is the date the invoice is raised.

CUSTOMER NAME AND ADDRESS: If the goods are being sent to an address other than the billing address, include the shipping address as well.

PRODUCT INFORMATION: Include columns for code, description, materials, unit price, quantity and subtotal.

SUBTOTALS, SHIPPING AND TAX: It is simplest, and acceptable, to add tax to the subtotal after shipping has been added.

PAYMENT TERMS: 30 days net is the most common.

PAYMENT INFORMATION: Don't forget to tell your customers how they can pay you. To make your own life easier you may wish to omit details of how to pay by cheque, in order to encourage payment by bank transfer.

COMPANY INFORMATION: It is a legal requirement that your company information is shown on your invoices, including company registration number and company address.

VAT NUMBER: If you are VAT registered, it is also a legal requirement that this number appears on your invoices.

SAMPLE INVOICE

Smith & Bloggs
Unit 1, The Studios
123 High Street
Anywheresville
AY1 2SV
Tel: 012 345 6789
jane@smithandbloggs.biz
www.smithandbloggs.biz

To:
Accounts Department
The Jewellery Shop
456 High Street
Anytown
AT8 5JS

Invoice No. 01736
Date
Customer ref: P0-00098

Code	Description	Unit Price	Quantity	Subtotal
0522	One-off necklace, leaf shapes with squares 50" long	£1,228	1	£1,228
SFNL01-S	'Sunflower' necklace	£76	2	£152
SFBL01-S	'Sunflower' bracelet	£49	2	£98
SFER01-S	'Sunflower' earrings	£24	2	£48

Net amount	£1,526.00
Shipping	£7.50
Total net	£1,533.50
VAT @ 20%	£306.70
Total due and payable	**£1,840.20**

Terms: 30 Days Net

Payment: Please pay by bank transfer into the following account:

The Small Jewellery Company Limited

Sort code: 10-10-10

Account number: 12345678

If paying by cheque, please make payable to The Small Jewellery Company Limited and post to the address above.

Smith & Bloggs is the trading name of The Small Jewellery Company Limited

Registered in England No. 12345678

Registered office 78 Company Street, Gemtown GT3 7HQ

VAT no. 012-345-678

SAMPLE PRO FORMA INVOICE

Smith & Bloggs
Unit 1, The Studios
123 High Street
Anywheresville
AY1 2SV
Tel: 012 345 6789
jane@smithandbloggs.biz
www.smithandbloggs.biz

To:
Accounts Department
The Jewellery Shop
456 High Street
Anytown
AT8 5JS

Pro Forma Invoice
Date
Customer ref: PO-00098

Code	Description	Unit Price	Quantity	Subtotal
0522	One-off necklace, leaf shapes with squares 50" long	£1,228	1	£1,228
SFNL01-S	'Sunflower' necklace	£76	2	£152
SFBL01-S	'Sunflower' bracelet	£49	2	£98
SFER01-S	'Sunflower' earrings	£24	2	£48

Net amount	£1,526.00
Shipping	£7.50
Total net	£1,533.50
VAT @ 20%	£306.70
Total due and payable	**£1,840.20**

Payment: Please pay by bank transfer into the following account:

The Small Jewellery Company Limited

Sort code: 10-10-10

Account number: 12345678

If paying by cheque, please make payable to The Small Jewellery Company Limited and post to the address above.

Smith & Bloggs is the trading name of The Small Jewellery Company Limited

Registered in England No. 12345678

Registered office 78 Company Street, Gemtown GT3 7HQ

VAT no. 012-345-678

Useful companies and websites

Metalcyberspace
www.metalcyberspace.com
This is a comprehensive listing of all things jewellery, from events to galleries to competitions. Wherever you are in the world, if you can't find what you're looking for here, go to Metalcyberspace!

Professional organizations

United States

American Craft Council
www.craftcouncil.org

Gemological Institute of America
www.gia.edu

Jewelers of America
www.jewelers.org

Society of North American Goldsmiths
www.snagmetalsmith.org

United Kingdom

Association for Contemporary Jewellery
www.acj.org.uk

Crafts Council
www.craftscouncil.org.uk

Federation of Small Businesses
www.fsb.org.uk

The National Association of Jewellers
www.naj.co.uk

Australia

Jewellers and Metalsmiths Group of Australia, NSW
www.jmgansw.org.au

Jewellers and Metalsmiths Group of Australia, QLD
www.visualartist.info/JMGQ

Jewellers and Metalsmiths Group of Australia, WA
www.jmgawa.com.au

Fairs and exhibitions

Trade fairs

Listed below are just a few of the dozens of jewellery trade fairs that take place around the world each year and which have been chosen for inclusion here because they offer some scope for individual designer/makers or those exhibiting for the first time. There are also plenty of bigger fairs such as Baselworld (www.baselworld.com) and JCK (lasvegas.jckonline.com) which are geared towards big brands and manufacturers; you may want to consider these further down the line depending on where you plan to take your business.

NY NOW (New York)
www.nynow.com
This is a major trade fair for the home, lifestyle and gift market. Of particular interest for designer/makers is a section called 'Handmade Designer Maker' which features hand-crafted products across a range of disciplines including jewellery. For more details on this section go to www.nynow.com/handmade/designer-maker.

Inhorgenta (Munich)
www.inhorgenta.com
This international trade fair for jewellery, watches, design, gemstones and technology boasts over 1,000 exhibitors spread across six exhibition halls. The 'Contemporary Design' hall is renowned for featuring many of Europe's most innovative designer/makers, both new and established.

International Jewellery London (London)
www.jewellerylondon.com
This is the main event in the UK jewellery industry calendar and features over 500 exhibitors from around the world including designers, manufacturers, gemstone dealers and tool/equipment suppliers. It is a common first trade fair for UK makers.

Jewellery Watch at Spring Fair International (Birmingham)
www.jewelleryandwatchbirmingham.com
A show within a show, Jewellery and Watch is part of the

mammoth Spring Fair International which includes a broad range of companies selling everything from stationery to garden furniture. Within Jewellery and Watch is a section geared towards designer jewellers so it is well worth looking into.

Retail fairs

The following is a selection of some of the more established retail fairs where jewellery designers can sell directly to the public. There are hundreds of shows taking place annually around the world; your local professional association (see 'professional associations' above) should be able to provide you with information about shows in your immediate area. (And don't forget to check the 'events' section on Metalcyberspace!)

NETHERLANDS
Sieraad (Amsterdam)
www.sieraadartfair.com

UNITED KINGDOM
Desire (London and surrounding areas)
www.desirefair.com

Great Northern Contemporary Craft Fair (Manchester)
www.greatnorthernevents.co.uk

Goldsmiths' Fair (London)
www.goldsmithsfair.co.uk

UNITED STATES
American Crafts Council shows (Baltimore, Atlanta, St Paul, San Francisco)
www.craftcouncil.org

Selling online
Website builders

www.godaddy.com
www.moonfruit.com
www.shopify.com
www.sitebuilder.com
www.squarespace.com
www.weebly.com

www.wix.com
www.wordpress.com

Online marketplaces

www.aftcra.com
www.artfire.com
www.bonanza.com
www.dawanda.com
www.ebay.com
www.etsy.com
www.storenvy.com
www.supermarkethq.com

Accounting / stock management

inFlow
www.inflowinventory.com
Inventory management system

KashFlow
www.kashflow.com
Online accounting software for small businesses with stock management functionality

Merchant accounts

Barclaycard Merchant Services (UK)
www.barclaycard.co.uk/business

Helcim (US/Canada)
www.helcim.com

Payline Data (US)
www.paylinedata.com

Payment Depot (US)
www.paymentdepot.com

Streamline (UK)
www.streamline.com

Shipping

Brinks
www.brinks.com
www.brinksglobal.com
Specialist shipping for diamonds and valuables

FedEx
www.fedex.com
International shipping service

Malca Amit
www.malca-amit.com
Specialist courier for jewellery and precious metals

Royal Mail
www.royalmail.com
The 'Special Delivery' service is a popular choice for UK jewellers

United States Postal Service
www.usps.com
The 'Registered Mail' service is popular with jewellers in the US

UPS
www.ups.com
International shipping service

Worldnet International
www.worldnet-intl.com
Secure shipping for fashion and luxury goods

Packaging

Ch. Dahlinger
www.dahlinger.com

Noble Packaging
www.noblepack.com

Rio Grande
www.riogrande.com

Sodem
www.sodem.de

To Be Packaging
www.tobe.it

Westpack
www.westpack.com

Business cards / postcards

Moo
www.moo.com

Vistaprint
www.vistaprint.com

Zazzle
www.zazzle.com

Business advice

General

B Plans
www.bplans.co.uk
Free business plan templates

Designing an MBA
designinganmba.com
Business thinking for designers and makers

Startup Donut
www.startupdonut.co.uk
Advice for new businesses

Design protection

ACID (Anti Copying In Design)
www.acid.uk.com

Government websites
Australia: www.business.gov.au
Europe: ec.europa.eu/internal_market/eu-go/index_en.htm
UK: www.gov.uk
USA: www.irs.gov/businesses/small

Workshop space (London)

Cockpit Arts
www.cockpitarts.com

Craft Central
www.craftcentral.org.uk

The Goldsmiths' Centre
www.goldsmiths-centre.org

Pullens Yards
www.pullensyards.co.uk

The Workspace Group
www.workspacegroup.co.uk

Hallmarking offices (UK)

Birmingham Assay Office
www.theassayoffice.co.uk

Edinburgh Assay Office
www.edinburghassayoffice.co.uk

London Assay Office
www.thegoldsmiths.co.uk

Sheffield Assay Office
www.assayoffice.co.uk

Bibliography

Eidelberg, Martin (ed.), *Messengers of Modernism: American Studio Jewelry 1940–1960*, Montreal: Montreal Museum of Decorative Arts in association with Flammarion, 1996 (ISBN 978 2 080135 933)

Harvey, Greg, *Excel 2013 All-In-One for Dummies*, Hoboken, NJ: John Wiley & Sons, 2013 (ISBN 978 1 118510 100)

Jenkins, David Ellis, *Financial Decision Making*, ICSA study text, London: ICSA Publishing, 2012 (ISBN 978 1 860724 879)

Jolly, Adam (ed.), *The Handbook of European Brand Rights Management*, London: Kogan Page Limited, 2011 (ISBN 978 0 749461 447)

Keenan and Riches' Business Law, 11th edn, London: Pearson, 2013 (ISBN 978 1 447922 933)

Mattacks, Keith, *Strategy in Practice*, ICSA study text, London: ICSA Publishing, 2011 (ISBN 978 1 860724 558)

Mintzberg, Henry, *Managing*, Harlow: Financial Times / Prentice Hall, 2009 (ISBN 978 0 273709 305)

Parks, Steve, *Start Your Business Week By Week: How to Plan and Launch Your Successful Business – One Step at a Time*, Harlow: Pearson Education Limited, 2005 (ISBN 978 0 273694 472)

Price, Barclay, *Running a Workshop: Basic Business for Craftspeople*, London: Crafts Council, 1997 (ISBN 978 1 870145 739)

Richey, Marlene, *Profiting By Design: A Jewelry Maker's Guide to Business Success*, Attleboro, MA: MJSA Press, 2008 (ISBN 978 0 971349 599)

Index